Appomattox Court House

M000094653

**Appomattox Court House
National Historical Park, Virginia**

Produced by the
Division of Publications
Harpers Ferry Center
National Park Service

U.S. Department of the Interior
Washington, D.C.

National Park Handbooks support management programs and promote the understanding and enjoyment of the more than 380 parks in the National Park System. The National Park Service cares for these special places saved by the American people so that all may enjoy our heritage. Handbooks are sold at parks and can be purchased by mail from the Superintendent of Documents, U.S. Government Printing Office, Stop SSOP, Washington, DC 20402-0001 or through the Internet at bookstore.gpo.gov. This is handbook number 160.

Library of Congress Cataloging-in-Publication Data
Appomattox Court House: Appomattox Court House National Historical Park, Virginia/produced by the Division of Publications, National Park Service.
    p. cm. — (National park handbook series; 160)
Includes bibliographical references and index.
ISBN 0-912627-70-0
    1. Appomattox Campaign, 1865. 2. Appomattox Court House National Historical Park (Va.). I. United States. National Park Service. Division of Publications. II. Handbook (United States. National Park Service. Division of Publications); 160.

E477.67 .A75 2002
973.7'38−dc21   2002276257

Introduction

As the photographs on the preceding pages seem to suggest, Appomattox Court House is an unpretentious village on a windswept ridge, a quiet spot that maintains its importance with patient dignity. Unlike such well-worn tourist paths as Fredericksburg, Vicksburg, or Gettysburg, where history is a mantle proudly worn, Appomattox seems to make a determined effort to keep its importance in perspective.

Thirteen of the buildings that existed in April 1865 remain in the village today, while nine other structures, including the McLean house, where the surrender actually took place, have been reconstructed on the original sites. But for the absence of normal village sounds—men and women going about their daily routines, children playing, an occasional wagon lumbering by, and the noise from chickens and livestock—it seems almost like a step back into the 19th century.

The surrender of Robert E. Lee to Ulysses S. Grant at Appomattox Court House led to the conclusion of the bloodiest war the United States has ever and, it is hoped, will ever experience. The victory of the Union over the Confederacy sealed the fate of the institution of slavery and ended the question of secession. The Civil War fundamentally changed the political, economic, and social landscape of the United States, and while the expansion of civil liberties envisioned in the 14th and 15th Amendments, which the outcome of the war helped to bring about, was not realized until a century later, the country had taken a giant step toward achieving the "more perfect Union" conceived by the Constitution eight decades earlier. The inherent conflict between the Declaration of Independence's proclamation that "all men are created equal" and the Constitution's acknowledgment of the institution of slavery had been resolved. The extension of civil and human rights launched by the end of the war continues to affect the social and political fabric of the country.

In 2009 the United States will begin to commemorate the sesquicentennial of the Civil War. In anticipation of that event, the National Park Service is updating its interpretive handbook series to incorporate the results of current scholarship on the history and meaning of the war. In this handbook, which replaces an earlier version produced more than 20 years ago, the perspectives of three eminent historians—Edward Ayers, Gary Gallagher, and David Blight—place the events of April 9, 1865, in the context of the Civil War era. Through their essays we see afresh the causes of the war, the last days of the Confederacy as Lee struggled from Petersburg to Appomattox, and the implications of Appomattox for the post-war generation.

Part 1

The Road to Disunion and War

Slavery, Economics, and Constitutional Ideals

By Edward L. Ayers

Abraham Lincoln, seen here a month before his second inaugural, shared many of the racial prejudices of his day. He was willing to compromise with the South on many issues involving slavery to preserve the Union and the Constitution, but he refused to compromise his opposition to the extension of slavery into the territories.

Preceding pages: *A "Slave Auction at the South" from the July 13, 1861, issue of* Harper's Weekly. *The engraving was developed from a sketch by artist Theodore Davis, who witnessed several such scenes while traveling with William Howard Russell, a reporter for the* London Times, *on a tour through the Confederacy early in the war.*

Everyone knows Appomattox Court House as the place where the Civil War ended, where Lt. Gen. Ulysses S. Grant and Gen. Robert E. Lee signed the document that ended the fighting between the largest of the Civil War armies. This is where the 30,000 remaining soldiers of the Army of Northern Virginia laid down their arms, where Union soldiers treated their recent opponents with respect, where soldiers tried to show Americans how they could have peace with dignity after four years of brutal war.

As we think about endings, however, it is also useful to think about beginnings. That is what President Abraham Lincoln did in his Second Inaugural Address, delivered just five weeks before the surrender at Appomattox and his own assassination soon thereafter. All knew, he said, reflecting sadly and thoughtfully on how the Civil War came about, that slavery was, "somehow," the cause. In that "somehow," however, lay puzzles, contradictions, and questions. The connections between slavery and the Civil War have concerned Americans ever since the events at Appomattox.

Time after time, between the 1780s and the 1860s, slavery provided both the fuel and the spark for a series of confrontations in Congress, in the Supreme Court, and in the Presidency; angry debate broke out in newspapers, books, and churches; it broke out in Virginia, Boston, and Kansas. Slavery unleashed the harshest words, the hardest feelings, and the most desperate acts in American history.

Nevertheless, anomalies and complexities marked the role of slavery in dividing the North and South. By 1861, after all, slavery had existed for two centuries in what became the United States. The slave economy grew stronger in the 1850s, flourishing as never before. Only a quarter of southern whites owned slaves and that proportion declined as the years passed. Only a small fraction of northern whites ever joined the abolitionists. Some of the largest slaveholders in the South voted against secession and many northern men voted against the Republicans in 1860 and in every election during the war. (Women were not allowed to vote until the adoption of the 19th Amendment to the Constitution in 1920.)

Dwelling on these complexities, some people have insisted that the Civil War could not have turned on slavery. It must have been about competing constitutional ideals or economic self interest, about politics or the personality of leaders. Others assert that war and emancipation were inevitable, or that slavery simply could not survive American progress and ideals. Many have questioned why such a large portion of the population, North and South, would be willing to fight for an institution in which they had no personal stake.

The simple arguments ignore too much. The challenge is to understand how a fundamental yet long-contained conflict suddenly exploded into a war that surprised everyone with its scale and consequences. The challenge is to understand the deaths of more than 620,000 people in a catastrophic war that few sought but many fought, a war that brought a great good in the destruction of slavery.

By the time of the American Revolution, slavery had become deeply entrenched in North America. Slaveholders helped found the new nation and demanded accommodation to slavery in the Constitution. With the white population booming and American participation in the international slave trade abolished after 1808, there was hope that slavery would meet the same fate in the South as in the North: a gradual fading, without deep social dislocation or serious financial loss to slaveholders.

Reassuring expectations of the painless demise of slavery died soon after the nation's founding. Slaveholders pushed into new lands to raise cotton, and the burgeoning demand for slaves gave the institution a new profitability even in states that could not

	Population of Appomattox County 1850 & 1860		
Census Year		1850	1860
Whites		4209	4118
Slaves		4799	4600
Free Blacks		185	171
Total		9193	8889

The overall population of Appomattox County declined during the 1850s, as this chart shows, but the county fared well economically. In 1860 the county's 4,600 slaves and 171 freedmen accounted for more than 53 percent of the total population. Most blacks stayed in the county after the war, as evidenced by the 1870 census, which showed the black population at 4,536. Many freedmen worked as servants or sharecroppers in the postwar years. Others were farmers owning land, or tradesmen with their own businesses (such as blacksmiths, shoemakers, wheelwrights, and coopers).

Slave sale broadside from Richmond, Virginia.

William Lloyd Garrison considered slavery "utterly evil" and fought against it uncompromisingly through the pages of The Liberator, *the militant antislavery newspaper he founded in 1831 and continued to publish for the next 34 years, until the ratification of the 13th Amendment ended slavery.*

grow the valuable fiber. As the United States government purchased or seized land from the American Indians, the French, the Spanish, and Mexico, the boundaries of the United States seemed to dissolve, promising a nation that would cover all of North America and the Caribbean. The number of slave states and free states grew at an equally torrid pace.

The United States Constitution could not contain the conflicts that resulted over the expansion of slavery. The document's three-fifths and fugitive slave clauses came to antagonize the North without reassuring the South. The Founding Fathers avoided, finessed, or left murky issues that would emerge with increasing frequency over the next 50 years: the status of slavery in territories before they became states, the power of Congress to regulate the slave trade among states or to rid the District of Columbia of slavery, the authority to return slaves who escaped into free states, whether a state could peaceably leave the Union. These problems repeatedly came before Congress, dominating and disrupting entire sessions.

Debates over the admission of Missouri as a slave state in 1819 established the pattern for the debates and compromises to follow. "The North" and "the South" emerged as self-conscious places from those debates, uniting the new states of the Northwest with the states of New England, New York, and Pennsylvania against the new states of the Southwest with Virginia, the Carolinas, and Georgia. Missouri came into the Union with slavery at the same time as Maine came in without slavery, ensuring the balance between slave and free states, but Congress also prohibited slavery in all the lands north of the southern border of Missouri. When northern opponents of slavery flooded Congress with petitions, southern legislators forced the "Gag Rule" to prevent the acceptance of such documents, leading to charges of suppression of free speech.

Several remarkable years around 1830 amplified the conflict over slavery. In the Nullification Crisis, South Carolina fought with the Federal Government over the boundaries between state and national power, with tariff the subject of immediate dispute. At nearly the same time, slaves in Virginia, under the leadership of Nat Turner, launched a bloody raid on neighboring whites, striking terror throughout the

South and raising the stakes of the national debate. William Lloyd Garrison founded *The Liberator*, the first abolitionist newspaper to attract widespread attention, denouncing slavery as a sin and calling for its immediate end. In the next decade, both the Methodist and Baptist churches would separate over slavery, the first major American institutions to split. Slavery would no longer be merely a political issue but now stood as a moral division.

While only two percent of white northerners joined the abolitionist movement, many in the North came to view slavery as, at best, a crude social system, out of step with the times, economically inefficient, harmful to poorer whites, and corrupting of slaveholders who developed an inflated sense of themselves and their power. White southerners saw the North, in turn, as arrogant, greedy, and hypocritical, living far from the South, possessing no way to deal with the costs and consequences of their anti-slavery agitation. Black people in the North faced harsh discrimination and biting poverty, white southerners argued, and yet northerners dared criticize the South for a slavery it had inherited. Both regions came to view the other with distrust, expecting the worst and often finding it.

When the United States won a war with Mexico in 1848 many northerners worried that slavery, and the political power of the slave states, would vastly increase. The Wilmot Proviso, declaring that slavery could not be established in any territory the United States might win from Mexico as a result of the war, split Congress along sectional lines. Soon thereafter, the conflict over the admission of California as a free state tore at the nation.

After months of bitter struggle, Congress forged an elaborate truce in the Compromise of 1850. The Compromise left slavery in the District of Columbia alone but abolished the slave trade there. It provided a stronger law to capture fugitive slaves in the North and return them to their owners in the South but announced that Congress had no power to regulate the slave trade among the states. It admitted California as a free state but left undetermined the place of slavery in the other territories won from Mexico. The Compromise managed to infuriate both sides, making both feel they had lost. Harriet Beecher Stowe's novel, *Uncle Tom's Cabin*, inspired by the

Harriet Beecher Stowe first became aware of the evils of slavery from a domestic servant, a runaway slave, while living in Cincinnati, across the river from slave-holding Kentucky. She wrote Uncle Tom's Cabin *to protest the passage by Congress of the Fugitive Slave Act of 1850. The book, published in 1852, has been called the "greatest piece of artistic propaganda ever written by an American" and helped to intensify anti-slavery sentiment in the North in the years just before the outbreak of the Civil War.*

Chief Justice Roger B. Taney hoped to settle the slavery issue once and for all with his ruling in the Dred Scott case that only white persons could be citizens of the United States and that any measure, congressional or otherwise, barring slavery from U.S. territories was unconstitutional. The decision only served to intensify the divisions between North and South and became one of the principal causes of the Civil War.

battle over the fugitive slave law, sold 300,000 copies in 1852 and became the subject of the most popular play in American history, exposing many northerners to powerful antislavery emotions.

In 1854 Sen. Stephen A. Douglas of Illinois called for building a railroad across the continent to bind together the expanded United States. He proposed that the people of the new territories decide for themselves whether or not their states would permit slaves and slaveholders. Calling this policy "popular sovereignty," Douglas put it forward in the Kansas-Nebraska Bill and expected the slave issue to die down. Just the opposite happened: Kansas became the crucible of conflict between North and South. Antislavery forces in New England and New York sent abolitionist organizers and rifles to Kansas. Southerners, in turn, organized an expedition to reinforce their comrades. John Brown, a free-soil emigrant to Kansas retaliating for earlier violence, killed five proslavery men with razor-sharp broadswords. For good reason, the territory became known as "Bleeding Kansas." With insults flying in Congress, Rep. Preston Brooks of South Carolina searched out Sen. Charles Sumner of Massachusetts, who had delivered bitter speeches against slavery and personally insulted his family, and beat him senseless with a heavy rubber cane.

The Dred Scott case of 1857 brought the conflict over slavery into the Supreme Court. Chief Justice Roger B. Taney decreed that Congress had never held a constitutional right to restrict slavery in the territories and that therefore the Missouri Compromise of 1820 was invalid. White southerners exulted that they had been vindicated by the Dred Scott decision, that the Supreme Court was on their side, and that the North's demand for territories free of slavery was simply unconstitutional. Many northerners, however, sneered at the decision, which they saw as one more corrupt act by the forces of slavery. All of these events became chapters in a continuing story of conflict and distrust, driving the North and South farther apart.

Meanwhile the American political system shattered. Ever since the 1820s, through all the episodes of conflict, two national parties had held the nation together. Democrats and Whigs from the North and South cooperated with one another in order to win the Presidency and control the Congress; party leaders struck bargains and worked for compromise. But voters throughout the country grew disgusted with the two established parties, which seemed to grow more alike and less effectual with each passing year. While slavery played a role in that dissolution, the parties suffered from other problems, problems of leadership, economic policy, loss of direction, the challenges of immigration, and hard times. Massive numbers of Whigs abandoned the party, first for the "Know-Nothings," who blamed the nation's troubles on the immigrants pouring into the United States, and then for the Republican Party.

The Republicans were something new: a sectional party, explicitly devoted to the interests of white northerners. The Republicans blamed the country's turmoil on the Slave Power, a conspiracy of slaveholders in the highest reaches of national power. The Republicans called for the North to unite against the South, seizing the balance of power in Congress. The new northern party, a white man's party, called above all for the settlement of the western territories without slavery and without black people. In the debates between Republican Abraham Lincoln and Democrat Stephen A. Douglas in Illinois in 1858, the Republicans saw the most attractive presentation of their ideas and the emergence of a potential national leader. Lincoln combined a principled opposition to the spread of slavery with reassurances that he would not touch the institution where it had been established.

The Republicans distanced themselves from abolitionists, whom they portrayed as fanatics, but opposed slavery's expansion and its dominion in the highest reaches of power. The Democratic party remained the major party running against the Republicans, but it splintered into regional factions. Politicians of all sorts, suddenly finding themselves without a national constituency to worry about, played to the prejudices and vanity of their local audiences, indulging in the most extreme charges, inflaming North and South against one another.

In the fall of 1859 John Brown and a small force of antislavery men attacked the federal arsenal at Harpers Ferry, Virginia (now West Virginia), hoping to unleash a slave rebellion that would bring bondage to an end. Even hitherto moderate northerners and

Stephen A. Douglas believed "popular sovereignty" to be the answer to the slavery question and the way to keep sectional antagonisms from destroying the Union. He was wrong on both counts.

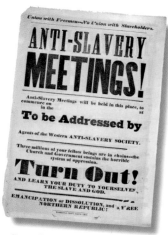

Broadside announcing a public lecture on the evils of slavery about 1855. Many such events were sponsored by abolitionist societies in the 1830s and 1840s.

John Brown was one of the most militant of abolitionists. His grandiose plans to free slaves won the moral and financial support of prominent New Englanders and led to vicious acts of violence and murder. The failure of his attack on the Harpers Ferry arsenal in 1859 resulted in his capture and subsequent hanging. On the day of his execution, he issued a final, prophetic statement: "I, John Brown, am now quite certain that the crimes of this guilty land will never be purged away but with blood."

southerners grew to distrust one another as they watched how the other side responded to Brown's raid. Many in the North could not hide their admiration for this man who acted rather than talked; many in the South found in John Brown confirmation of their worst suspicions of the North's bloodthirsty hatred of their countrymen.

The political conventions that met soon after Brown's execution to nominate candidates for President in 1860 arrayed themselves around the slavery issue. The Democrats split into northern and southern parties, the North behind Stephen Douglas and the South behind John C. Breckinridge. A new Constitutional Union party tried to mediate between North and South, running John Bell for President. The Republicans, after tumultuous struggle among various factions, turned to a moderate from a crucial and divided state: Abraham Lincoln of Illinois. Their platform announced that they would not disturb slavery where it already existed, but would not allow its spread. This stance resulted in the long-standing balance of power in Congress being shifted to the North.

By 1860, 400,000 slaveowners and 3,500,000 slaves worth $3 billion peopled a vast territory stretching from Delaware to Texas. Cotton accounted for an ever-increasing proportion of the exports of the United States, growing to more than half by 1860. Apologists devised ever more elaborate and aggressive defenses of slavery, no longer depicting bondage merely as a necessary evil or an unfortunate inheritance but rather as an instrument of God's will, a progressive force in the world, a means of civilizing and Christianizing Africans otherwise lost to heathenism.

The candidates of 1860 did not meet face to face, either in cooperation or in debate. Partisan newspapers portrayed opponents in the harshest light without fear of rebuttal. The South believed Lincoln to be a fervent abolitionist, though he was not. The North believed southerners were bluffing in their talk of secession, but they were not. The split in the Democratic Party gave Lincoln only 39 percent of the popular vote, and that came from northern states, but he triumphed easily in the electoral college.

The Republicans claimed to work within the political system, but southerners charged that Lincoln's supporters had violated an honored tradition of compromise necessary for the country's survival. The Republicans had built their campaign around anti-southern policies and rhetoric and did not seek the votes of southern men. The same states that had created the Union, southerners argued, could leave that Union when it turned against them and the South had every right, every incentive, to abandon a North that had expressed its rejection of the South in Lincoln's election. Indeed, Lincoln's election demonstrated that national elections could now be won without southern electoral votes. Deep South states quickly lined up behind South Carolina as secession rallies erupted across the region. Seven states left the Union by February 1861, when a new Confederacy named Jefferson Davis its President.

Many thousands of white southerners, some of them quite powerful and influential, resisted secession. Some argued that secession was treason. Others warned that the South was committing suicide. Others argued that slavery would be far safer within the Union than in a fragile new country bordered by an antagonistic United States. The opposition to secession proved especially strong in the upper South—in Virginia, North Carolina, Tennessee, Kentucky, and Maryland—all of which showed every sign of staying with the Union.

Northerners, too, were divided at the beginning of 1861. Many recent immigrants from Ireland and Germany viewed the conflict between the North and the South as none of their business. Northern Democrats, hating Lincoln and his policies, called for conciliation with the South. Men like former President John Tyler, as well as others from the large borderland that overlapped the North and the South across the middle of the nation, an area in which love of the Union and support for slavery easily coexisted, worked frantically, but fruitlessly, to find a compromise. In February 1861 the United States Senate came within just a few votes of passing a constitutional amendment protecting slavery forever and wherever the nation might ever expand. All the desperate compromises failed as the delegates of one Deep South state after another left the Senate and as Republicans steadfastly refused to give in.

President Lincoln told the South in his inaugural speech in March 1861 that he had no intention of touching slavery where it was already established,

The first notice of the adoption of the adoption of South Carolina's Ordinance of Secession appeared in the Charleston Mercury.

Jefferson Davis did not want to be president of the Confederacy but fulfilled his duties with unswerving devotion to the cause. "We have entered upon the career of independence," he said, "and it must be inflexibly pursued."

Alexis de Tocqueville, French statesman and writer, 1831

that he would not invade the region, that there would be no shedding of blood, and that he would not attempt to fill offices with men repugnant to local sensibilities. But he also warned that secession was illegal, "the essence of anarchy." It was his duty to maintain the integrity of the Federal Government, and to do so he had to "hold, occupy, and possess" Federal property in the states of the Confederacy. Lincoln, after delaying as long as he could for political and strategic ends, finally decided to send a relief expedition to Fort Sumter in Charleston, South Carolina, where food was running out for the besieged Federal garrison there.

Jefferson Davis and his government proclaimed that any attempt to supply the fort would be in and of itself an act of war, a violation of the territorial integrity of the new Confederacy. On April 12, at 4:30 in the morning, Gen. Pierre G. T. Beauregard opened fire on the fort to drive out the Federal soldiers. Southerners, even those who resented South Carolina for precipitating the war, agreed that they had no choice but to come to that state's aid if the North raised a hand against their fellow southerners. President Lincoln felt he had no choice but to call out militia to put down secession. When he did, Virginia, Tennessee, Arkansas, and North Carolina quickly joined their fellow slaveholding states. Kentucky and Maryland, despite the presence of strong advocates of secession, considered the matter and then, under Federal military threat, remained in the Union.

All the events that brought on the Civil War, then, turned around slavery. By 1861 slavery had become a fundamental feature of the American political, economic, and religious landscape. Slavery was growing ever stronger, intertwining itself ever more tenaciously into a prosperous South of railroads, telegraphs, newspapers, and towns. Southern secessionists announced that slavery stood as the "cornerstone" of their new slaveholding republic, one of the richest nations in the world from the moment of its birth. Slavery defined the only difference that mattered enough to destroy the Union. Yet the complexities and contradictions remained deep.

No intractable differences between an industrial and agrarian society drove the North and South apart; no debate over a tariff played an important role after the 1830s. Slavery and the regional division of labor benefited white people in both the North and the South. Even in New England, the home of the most fervent abolitionists, thousands of mill-workers depended on southern cotton for their livelihood. The great majority of white people in the United States thought about slavery only when forced to. Politicians spent most of their time on issues that had nothing to do with slavery. At the moment of crisis, Confederate leaders rallied Southerners not around slavery but around family, home, and Constitution. Union leaders rallied northerners not against slavery but around economy, democracy, and nation.

That "somehow" in Abraham Lincoln's second inaugural address expressed the sense in which slavery caused the Civil War, not as a moral crusade or a principled protection of abstract constitutional rights for the South, but as the factor that had led to broken political compromises, cultural and social differences, and mutual distrust between the North and the South. The North and the South acted from anger built up over generations. Emotion and thought had become merged, with memories of events from the last four decades driving every decision. The Civil War began in expectation of easy victory over a detested enemy, a quick and satisfying ending to a long and frustrating argument. No one realized how long the war would last or the heartbreak, destruction, and lasting bitterness that would result from it.

1861

April 12-14
Bombardment and surrender of Fort Sumter, S.C.

April 15
President Lincoln calls for 75,000 volunteers to put down the rebellion.

April 19
Lincoln proclaims blockade of Southern coast.

July 21
First Battle of Manassas (Bull Run), Va.

August 10
Battle of Wilson's Creek, Mo.

A Massachusetts volunteer answers President Lincoln's call to fight by selling off his personal possessions to the highest bidder.

1862

February 6-16
Forts Henry and Donelson Campaign, Tenn.

March 6-8
Battle of Pea Ridge, Ark.

March 8-9
USS *Monitor* vs. CSS *Virginia* at Hampton Roads, Va.

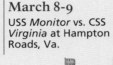

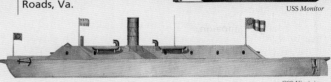

USS *Monitor*

CSS *Virginia*

March 23-June 9
Stonewall Jackson's Shenandoah Valley Campaign, Va.

April 6-7
Battle of Shiloh, Tenn.

April 24
Union fleet captures New Orleans, La.

May 31-June 1
Battle of Fair Oaks, Va.

June 1
Gen. Robert E. Lee assumes command of the Army of Northern Virginia.

June 25-July 1
Seven Days' Battles around Richmond, Va.

August 28-30
Second Battle of Manassas (Bull Run), Va.

September 14-17
Battles of South Mountain and Antietam (Sharpsburg), Md.

December 11-13
Battle of Fredericksburg, Va.

1863

January 1
President Lincoln issues Emancipation Proclamation.

First Reading of the Emancipation Proclamation based on the painting by Francis B. Carpenter

1864

April-May
Chancellorsville Campaign, Va.

June 3-July 13
Gettysburg Campaign, Pa.

March 29-July 4
Vicksburg Campaign, Miss.

August-September
Chickamauga Campaign, Ga.

October-November
Chattanooga Campaign, Tenn.

November 19
President Lincoln delivers Gettysburg Address.

May 5-6
Battle of the Wilderness, Va. Overland Campaign begins

May 7-September 2
Atlanta Campaign, Ga.

May 8-12
Battle of Spotsylvania Court House, Va.

June 1-3
Battle of Cold Harbor, Va.

June 18
Siege of Petersburg, Va., begins.

August 7-October 19
Sheridan's Shenandoah Valley Campaign, Va.

November 8
Abraham Lincoln is re-elected President.

November 15
Sherman begins his "March to the Sea" across Georgia.

November 30
Battle of Franklin, Tenn.

December 15-16
Battle of Nashville, Tenn.

December 21
Sherman reaches Savannah, leaving behind a 300-mile path of destruction 60 miles wide. He telegraphs Lincoln, offering the city as a Christmas present while the country begins to celebrate the holidays and wonder what the new year will bring.

Union mortar "Dictator" at the siege of Petersburg

1865

January 15
Fall of Fort Fisher, N.C., closes the port of Wilmington and eliminates the Confederacy's last link to the outside world.

January 31
U.S. House of Representatives passes 13th Amendment abolishing slavery.

February-March
Sherman advances through the Carolinas.

March 4
Lincoln's second inauguration.

Part 2

From Petersburg to Appomattox

An End and a New Beginning

By Gary W. Gallagher

When Union soldiers finally entered Richmond on April 3, 1865, they found much of the city in flames. "We are under the shadow of ruins," a New York World *reporter wrote after touring the ruined city. "From the pavements where we walk...stretches a vista of devastation.... The wreck, the loneliness seem interminable." Some 900 buildings were destroyed by fires set by retreating Confederates.*

Preceding pages: *A Federal wagon train leaves Petersburg to join in the pursuit of Robert E. Lee's Army of Northern Virginia, then slogging westward toward a little crossroad village named Appomattox Court House.*

The winter of 1865 found citizens of the United States and the Confederacy looking toward another round of military campaigning in the spring. Nearly 600,000 men had perished in a conflict whose scope and fury had far surpassed anything predicted by even the most pessimistic observers in 1861. Although no one knew when the fighting might cease, and Lt. Gen. Ulysses S. Grant's Union forces and Gen. Robert E. Lee's Army of Northern Virginia had been locked in a siege outside Richmond and Petersburg for more than six months, recent political and military developments clearly favored the Union. In November 1864 Republican success in the national elections virtually assured that the North would press the war vigorously. Victories on the battlefield followed the elections, with Maj. Gen. George H. Thomas's forces smashing Gen. John Bell Hood's Confederate Army of Tennessee at Nashville and Maj. Gen. William Tecumseh Sherman carrying out his famous "March to the Sea" before turning north into the Carolinas. Although many Confederates had lost heart by the beginning of 1865, a majority remained committed to the idea of southern independence. Typical was Kate Cumming, a nurse in Mobile, Alabama, who acknowledged the hardships confronting the Confederacy but vowed continued resistance. "Although woe and desolation stare at us every way we turn, the heart of the patriot is as firm as ever, and determined that, come what may, he will never yield," wrote Cumming, who hoped "the time is not far distant when triumphant peace will spread her wings over this now distracted land."

A number of Confederates took heart in early February when they learned that commissioners from the two sides would discuss a possible end to the war. The meeting took place on February 3 at Hampton Roads, Virginia, aboard the U.S. vessel *River Queen*, with President Abraham Lincoln heading the Union delegation and Vice President Alexander H. Stephens

> *"We cannot afford to underrate him and the army he now commands. That man will fight us every day and every hour till the end of the war."*

James Longstreet, lieutenant general, First Corps, Army of Northern Virginia, C.S.A., on Ulysses S. Grant

the Confederate contingent. It quickly became apparent that each side's minimal demands precluded any substantive agreement. Lincoln insisted on reunion and emancipation (the United States Congress had just passed the 13th Amendment, which, upon ratification, would end slavery), and Jefferson Davis had instructed Stephens to press for an end to the war on the basis of Confederate independence. Lincoln reported laconically to the House of Representatives that "the conference ended without result." Disappointed Confederates tended to ascribe bad faith to the North, as when a North Carolina woman bitterly observed that all Lincoln offered was "submission, entirely, utterly, & abject to the U.S., then an adoption of the new & remarkable Constitution of their country just passed by the Federal Congress, one clause of which is the Abolition of Slavery...."

Most people understood that armies rather than peace commissioners would decide the war's outcome. They also looked to the Virginia theater of operations for a final verdict. Robert E. Lee and the Army of Northern Virginia had long since become the primary national rallying point for most Confederates, engendering hope for independence so long as they remained in the field. A member of Britain's Parliament named Thomas Conolly, while on a visit to Richmond late in the war, commented on the degree of trust invested in Lee, describing him as "the idol of his soldiers & the Hope of His Country." "[T]he prestige which surrounds his person & the almost fanatical belief in his judgement and capacity," added Conolly in his diary, "...is the one idea of an entire people." Northern leaders took a similar view of Lee's importance. Radical Republican Sen. Charles Sumner of Massachusetts commented in mid-February that he had "for a long time been sanguine that, when Lee's army is out of the way, the whole Rebellion will disappear." But should Lee's army remain "in fighting condition," thought Sumner, "there is still hope for the rebels, & the unionists of the South are afraid to show themselves." Secretary of War Edwin M. Stanton, in a conversation with Sumner in February, agreed that peace would come "only when Lee's army is beaten, captured or dispersed." Stanton predicted victory sometime before May.

From the Rapidan to Petersburg: The 1864 Overland Campaign

In the spring of 1864, when Ulysses S. Grant took command of all Union armies and joined George G. Meade and his Army of the Potomac in the field, neither North nor South controlled more or less territory in Virginia than it had at the beginning of the war. Robert E. Lee's Army of Northern Virginia still stood between Washington and Richmond. Grant was determined to break this stalemate, and he reasoned that it could only be done by destroying the Confederate Army. So when he crossed the Rapidan River west of Fredericksburg on May 4, 1864, he had decided to attack Lee again and again until the Confederates were either destroyed or captured.

The first engagement took place in a tangled, densely overgrown stretch of country west of Fredericksburg known as the Wilderness. For two days the armies fought, giving and gaining little ground. The armies then separated and Grant began to move. But instead of heading back across the Rapidan as other Federal commanders had done, he sidestepped to the left and headed southeast, hoping to place the Union Army between Richmond and Lee. Lee would have no choice but to attack Grant, for the loss of the Confederate capital would be a psychological blow the Confederacy could ill survive.

Lee managed to get ahead of the Federals and establish his army at Spotsylvania Court House. This forced Grant to do the attacking, and the fighting continued for 12 days. Yet it was all inconclusive; no one ad-

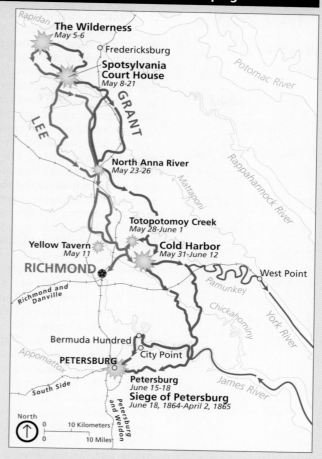

vanced and no one retreated. Grant just kept sidestepping to the southeast while Lee tried to stay between him and Richmond.

As the two armies moved toward Richmond they almost daily would bump into each other and small fights would flare up. Of these skirmishes, the clashes at North Anna and Totopotomoy Creek were the costliest in men and materiel. From May 31-June 12, the two armies faced each other at Cold Harbor in the last major engagement of

the Overland Campaign. By June 12, after several costly attacks failed to dislodge the Confederates, Grant realized he could not get at Lee or Richmond by direct assault, so he took his armies across the James River toward the important rail and road junction of Petersburg. Union delays enabled the Confederates to come up in full force, compelling Grant to lay siege to Petersburg—a siege that would last until April 2, 1865, when Lee was forced to abandon both Petersburg and Richmond.

Abraham Lincoln's second inaugural address confirmed the importance of recent Union military successes but avoided setting any timetable for victory. "The progress of our arms, upon which all else chiefly depends, is as well known to the public as to myself; and it is, I trust, reasonably satisfactory and encouraging to all," stated the President on March 4. "With high hope for the future," he cautioned, "no prediction in regard to it is ventured." Lincoln hoped and prayed that "this mighty scourge of war may speedily pass away. Yet, if God wills that it continue, until all the wealth piled by the bond-man's two hundred and fifty years of unrequited toil shall be sunk, and until every drop of blood drawn with the lash, shall be paid by another drawn with the sword, as was said three thousand years ago, so still it must be said, 'the judgments of the Lord, are true and righteous altogether.'"

Two days before Lincoln's speech, Robert E. Lee had proposed to Ulysses S. Grant that they discuss a military convention to stop the bloodshed. Lee acted in response to a suggestion from Lt. Gen. James Longstreet, commander of the Army of Northern Virginia's First Corps, that Grant might be receptive to such an overture. Longstreet recently had met with Maj. Gen. E.O.C. Ord, who headed the Union Army of the James, to discuss issues relating to prisoners of war, and in the course of their talks the two men resolved that it would be worthwhile for Lee and Grant to get together. Ord later recalled that Longstreet said Lee "considered the cause of the South hopeless.... That it was a great crime against the Southern people and Army for the chief Generals to continue to lead their men to hopeless and unnecessary butchery...." Jefferson Davis, averred Ord quoting Longstreet, "was the great obstacle to peace." Lee's communication to Grant avoided any reference to surrender (President Davis would not have allowed that), but it left no doubt that its author sought to stop the slaughter: "Sincerely desiring to leave nothing untried which may put an end to the calamities of war, I propose to meet you at such convenient time and place as you may designate, with the hope that upon an interchange of views, it may be found practicable to submit the subjects of controversy between the belligerents to a convention of the Kind mentioned." Grant replied to Lee on March 4, declining the meeting on the grounds that he lacked the authority to deal "on the subject proposed." "Such authority," noted Grant, "is vested in the President of the United States alone."

Lee faced an increasingly desperate situation. His soldiers in the Richmond-Petersburg lines lacked sufficient food and fodder. Desertions increased daily. Maj. Gen. Philip H. Sheridan's victory over Lt. Gen. Jubal A. Early's badly outnumbered Confederates at the battle of Waynesboro, Virginia, on March 2 had ended significant fighting in the Shenandoah Valley and freed Sheridan's formidable cavalry divisions to join Grant. Lee met with Jefferson Davis in early March, explaining the plight of his army and offering little hope that Richmond and Petersburg could be defended much longer. Davis insisted that victory and independence still might be wrested from a dismal situation, and Lee turned to the problem of how best to extricate his army from Grant's strangling grip. If freed to maneuver in the field, he saw some hope in cooperating with Gen. Joseph E. Johnston's force to stop Sherman's army in North Carolina. Lee settled on a plan involving an attack against a portion of Grant's army at Petersburg. If successful, this might oblige Grant to shorten his lines, allowing Lee to reinforce Johnston with part of the Army of Northern Virginia. Should the united Confederates defeat Sherman, Lee then would return to Virginia to deal with Grant. On March 23, Johnston informed Lee that "Sherman's course cannot be hindered by the small force I have." Lee's supply lines to the south thus lay exposed. Sheridan's command soon would add its numbers to Grant's host. Lee concluded that he must act quickly. He selected Maj. Gen. John B. Gordon, a 33-year-old Georgian who led Stonewall Jackson's old Second Corps, to supervise the assault that, if successful, would trigger the rest of the plan to defeat Sherman and Grant in turn. The attack was set to commence before dawn on March 25.

Gordon chose Fort Stedman, a strong point on the right of Grant's siege lines at Petersburg, as his target. With approximately 11,500 men in his immediate command and assurances that another 8,000 infantry and a division of cavalry would be available to exploit any advantage, Gordon launched his attack just before dawn on what one officer described as "the cool,

Cavalry Soldier *by Winslow Homer, one of the special artists hired by* Harper's Weekly *to record the events of the war. It has been said of Homer, whose unretouched field sketches appear occasionally on the following pages, that "no other artist left so authentic a record of how the Civil War soldier really looked and acted."*

Continued on page 36

Lt. Gen. Ulysses S. Grant

"I can't spare this man. He fights!" That's how Abraham Lincoln once characterized his 42-year-old general in chief, Ulysses S. Grant, who oversaw the operations of all Union forces in the Appomattox Campaign and whose dogged pursuit of Lee's troops after the fall of Richmond and Petersburg led to the surrender of the Army of Northern Virginia. George G. Meade, a 49-year-old Pennsylvanian, commanded the Army of the Potomac during the campaign, as he had since June 1863, but he was largely overshadowed by Grant's presence. Edward O. C. Ord, a 46-year-old Marylander, had taken command of the Army of the James in January 1865 after recovering from a wound received in the previous year's fighting around Richmond. Philip H. Sheridan, who commanded four cavalry divisions as well as supporting infantry during the campaign, was one of Grant's favorite officers. His driving personality and aggressive tactics in harassing Lee's army during the pursuit led the 34-year-old Sheridan to tell Grant after the Battle of Sailor's Creek: "If the thing is pressed I think Lee will surrender." Informed of this, Lincoln telegraphed Grant: "Let the thing be pressed."

Maj. Gen. George G. Meade

Maj. Gen. Philip H. Sheridan

Maj. Gen. Edward O. C. Ord

Lt. Gen. James Longstreet

Beloved by the soldiers he led, Robert E. Lee had commanded the Army of Northern Virginia since June 1862. In late-January 1865, at the age of 58, he had been made general in chief of all the armies of the failing Confederacy. Even then he knew that it was only a matter of time before "our present lines must be abandoned." Lee's senior lieutenant was 44-year-old James Longstreet, commander of the First and (since the death of A. P. Hill on April 2) Third corps. He has been called "a superb battlefield commander with great tactical skills" and led the advance units of Lee's retreating army. John B. Gordon, a 33-year-old Georgian, commanded the Second Corps and remnants of Richard Anderson's Corps after the Battle of Sailor's Creek. His troops acted as the army's rear guard during most of the campaign and made the final assault at Appomattox Court House on April 9 in an attempt to open an escape route to the west. The Army of Northern Virginia's chief cavalry officer was Fitzhugh Lee, the 29-year-old nephew of Robert E. Lee. He and much of his cavalry eluded the tightening Federal noose on April 9 and surrendered in Farmville a few days later.

Maj. Gen. John B. Gordon

Maj. Gen. Fitzhugh Lee

Gen. Robert E. Lee

frosty morning" of the 25th. Confederates overran Fort Stedman, capturing nearly a thousand prisoners and seeking to enlarge their breakthrough by moving north and south along the Union lines. But the Federals reacted swiftly, mounting several counterattacks that recaptured Fort Stedman, liberated many comrades taken in the first rush of Confederate success, and drove Gordon's men back to the southern lines. Gordon's reminiscences included a typically overblown passage about the action: "This last supreme effort to break the hold of General Grant upon Petersburg and Richmond was the expiring struggle of the Confederate giant, whose strength was nearly exhausted and whose limbs were heavily shackled by the most onerous conditions." Grant chose more restrained language in his own memoirs: "This effort of Lee's cost him about four thousand men, and resulted in their killing, wounding and capturing about two thousand of ours." In fact, nearly 3,000 Confederates had fallen in a battle that marked the last major offensive gasp of the Army of Northern Virginia.

Perhaps equally important, Union forces followed up their repulse of Gordon's assault with a series of probing movements that seized crucial sections of the Confederate picket lines at Petersburg. Grant fully appreciated the importance of these successes, which, he explained, "gave us but a short distance to charge over when our attack came to be made a few days later." Lee also understood what had been lost on the 25th. "I fear now it will be impossible to prevent a junction between Grant and Sherman," he told Jefferson Davis on March 26, "nor do I deem it prudent that this army should maintain its position until the latter shall approach too near."

By the time Lee sent this gloomy evaluation to Davis, Grant had issued the orders that would settle the fate of Richmond's and Petersburg's defenders. The Federals had been pressing southward and westward for several months, stretching Lee's army to the limit and systematically cutting the roads and railroads over which Lee moved supplies to his beleaguered troops. On March 24, Grant instructed Maj. Gen. George G. Meade, commander of the Army of the Potomac, to prepare for an offensive that would turn the far Confederate right flank and sever the South Side Railroad, Lee's best available route to

reach Johnston's force in North Carolina. The Union Fifth and Second corps, under Maj. Gens. Gouverneur K. Warren and Andrew A. Humphreys respectively, would march toward the Boydton Plank Road and Confederate positions along the White Oak Road. The bulk of Ord's army would shift from north of the James to a supporting position near the far Union left. Sheridan's cavalry, fresh from its triumphs in the Shenandoah Valley, would strike west toward Dinwiddie Court House, a village just eight miles from the South Side Railroad. Grant told Sheridan that he "intended to close the war right here, with this movement . . . ." "I am glad to hear it," answered the diminutive but aggressive Sheridan, "and we can do it."

On March 29-31, Union infantry engaged Confederates along the Boydton and White Oak roads. Sheridan's cavalry reached Dinwiddie Court House on the evening of the 30th. Lee had anticipated Sheridan's movement, putting together a mobile force of roughly 10,000 men consisting of Maj. Gen. George E. Pickett's infantry division and a large body of cavalry under his nephew, Maj. Gen. Fitzhugh Lee. Pickett and Lee concentrated their units at Five Forks on the 30th and attacked Sheridan the next morning, forcing the Federals into a compact position near the courthouse before retiring to a defensive line near Five Forks.

The climactic action on the Confederate right occurred on April 1 at Five Forks, a strategic point on the road from Dinwiddie Court House to the South Side Railroad. Given charge of the Fifth Corps infantry as well as the cavalry divisions under Maj. Gen. Wesley Merritt, Sheridan devised a late-afternoon offensive. While Pickett and Fitzhugh Lee lounged behind their lines eating a leisurely meal, Federal attackers overran the Confederate position, inflicted more than 3,000 casualties at a cost of about 800 of their own, and opened the way to the vital railroad.

Grant had turned Lee's right flank and set the stage for the final act of a nine-month drama Lee had predicted the previous summer. In June 1864 as the Army of the Potomac and the Army of Northern Virginia faced each other east of Richmond after the battle of Cold Harbor, Lee had told Jubal Early that the Confederates could not afford to give up more

"For some time there has been the appearance of very uneasiness among our officers. All have a certain fear or dred of the coming campaign."

Thomas Mitchell, private, Phillips Georgia Legion, Army of Northern Virginia, C.S.A.

War Council on the *River Queen*

Toward the end of March 1865, Abraham Lincoln traveled down to City Point, Virginia, to talk strategy and peace terms with his general in chief, Ulysses S. Grant. The meeting took place on board the steamer *River Queen (below)*. William T. Sherman, who had come up from North Carolina to talk with Grant prior to the opening of the spring campaigns, and Rear Adm. David D. Porter, representing the Navy, were asked to join the meeting.

The talks began on March 27 and lasted two days. Everyone agreed that the war was almost over. According to Admiral Porter, the only one to keep detailed notes of the conference, the President "felt confident that we would be successful, and was willing that the enemy should capitulate on the most favorable terms.... His heart was tenderness throughout, and, as long as the rebels laid down their arms, he did not care how it was done. I do not know how far he was influenced by General Grant, but I presume, from their long conferences, that they must have understood each other perfectly.... Indeed, the President more than once told me what he supposed the terms would be: if Lee and Johnston surrendered, he considered the war ended, and that all the other rebel forces would lay down their arms at once. In this he proved to be right...."

G.P.A. Healy, an internationally known portrait painter, depicted the meeting on board the *River Queen* in a postwar painting he called "The Peacemakers" *(right)*. It is based on information supplied by Sherman, Grant, and Porter, who are shown, left to right, talking with Lincoln.

This bridge across the Appomattox River outside Petersburg, as well as the railroad cars and workshops, were destroyed by retreating Confederates. They were sketched by combat artist Alfred E. Waud of Harper's Weekly, *who accompanied Federal troops into Petersburg after its evacuation by Lee's army.*

ground: "We must destroy this army of Grant's before he gets to [the] James River," said Lee. "If he gets there, it will become a siege, and then it will be a mere question of time."

Time ran out for Petersburg's protectors on Sunday, April 2. Grant sought to deliver a knockout blow, ordering a wide-scale advance at first daylight along much of the Petersburg front. By mid-morning, Lee knew that Petersburg must be abandoned that day. Loss of Petersburg meant that the capital also would fall. "I advise that all preparation be made for leaving Richmond tonight," Lee wired the War Department in Richmond just after 10:30 a.m. Jefferson Davis received the message while in Saint Paul's Church, glanced at its contents, and hurried to the War Department. Fighting continued all day at Petersburg. Unremitting Union pressure west and southwest of the city eventually overwhelmed staunch defenders at Fort Gregg and elsewhere, but some Confederates hung on until nightfall. Lee spent the afternoon planning movements that would unite Confederate troops from north and south of the James for a march west. That night his soldiers began to shuffle out of Petersburg, and he rode Traveller northward across the temporary Battersea pontoon bridge spanning the Appomattox River.

Jefferson Davis and his entourage left Richmond by train for Danville that same evening, followed the next morning by the last Confederates defending the capital. One of those defenders later tried to convey what it had meant to abandon the city. "It was after sunrise of a bright morning when...we turned to take our last look at the old city for which we had fought so long & so hard," wrote artillerist Edward Porter Alexander. "It was a sad, a terrible & a solemn sight.... The whole river front seemed to be in flames, amid which occasional heavy explosions were heard, & the black smoke spreading & hanging over the city seemed to be full of dreadful portents. I rode on with a distinctly heavy heart & with a peculiar sort of feeling of orphanage."

Grant and Meade rode into Petersburg on the morning of April 3. Looking toward the Appomattox River, Grant saw large numbers of Confederate soldiers. "I did not have artillery brought up," he later explained, "because I was sure Lee was trying to make his escape, and I wanted to push immediately in pursuit. At all events I had not the heart to turn the artillery upon such a mass of defeated and fleeing men, and I hoped to capture them soon." Grant's attitude toward the Confederates mirrored that of his commander in chief. At a meeting with his top military leaders aboard the *River Queen* a week earlier at City Point, Virginia, Lincoln had expressed his strong desire to close the war as gently as possible. He asked whether the conflict could be ended without further bloodshed. Not if the rebels remained under arms in the field, answered General Sherman, who argued that responsibility for any additional deaths lay with Jefferson Davis and his government. But Lincoln persisted, repeating his desire to stop the killing and insisting that the enemy should be given liberal terms of surrender. "Let them surrender and go home," he remarked, "they will not take up arms again. Let them all go, officers and all, let them have their horses to plow with, and, if you like, their guns to shoot crows with.... We want these people to return to their allegiance and submit to the laws. Therefore, I say, give them the most liberal and honorable terms."

Many of Grant's soldiers took a considerably harder view of their long-time foes. A member of the 17th Maine Infantry spoke sarcastically of the Confederate retreat from Petersburg and of the extreme southern rights advocates who, in his view, had pre-

"The last two days have added long years to my life. I have cried until no more tears will come.... Through all this strain of anguish ran... the mad vain hope that Lee would yet make a stand somewhere [and] give us back our liberty."

Constance Cary, Richmond resident, April 4, 1865, after Federal occupation of the city

"*The...yells of drunken men, shouts of roving pillagers, wild cries of distress filled the air and made the night hideous.*"

Edward A. Pollard, editor, Richmond *Examiner*, on the aftermath of the evacuation of Richmond

cipitated the national crisis in the wake of Lincoln's election in 1860. By midnight on April 2, "the 'defenders of virgins fair and matrons grave' had made an inglorious flight and left the matrons and virgins to look out for themselves," recorded Private John W. Haley in his diary. "None are left to defend the city except some of the colored population and such whites as couldn't get away or who have sense enough to know that Yankees are human and not the ghouls we are represented to be by the Southern fire-eaters." Haley and his comrades knew that "Great things were done" on April 2. They turned in early that evening and "prepared to go in pursuit of the enemy" the next day.

Commanding the target of that pursuit, Robert E. Lee faced a daunting prospect. He must unite Confederate units that had occupied a 30-mile defensive arc around Richmond and Petersburg, secure provisions for his men and animals adequate to sustain them in an active campaign, and maintain enough of a lead over Grant's pursuing forces to allow the Army of Northern Virginia to turn south toward Johnston's army in North Carolina. He selected Amelia Court House, a hamlet due west of Petersburg on the Richmond and Danville Railroad, as the point of concentration. It was vital that the army be closed up before proceeding south along the railroad through Jetersville and Burkeville toward the Carolina border. Although historians disagree about Confederate numbers on April 2, the Army of Northern Virginia and miscellaneous units from the Richmond defenses (including a battalion of sailors) almost certainly approached, and perhaps exceeded, 60,000 men of all arms.

The morning of April 3 found four major Confederate columns plodding westward after a tiring night march. Farthest north, Lt. Gen. Richard S. Ewell's mixed force from the Richmond defenses traversed the James River and marched toward Genito Bridge, which spanned the Appomattox River a few miles northeast of Amelia Court House. Next in line to the south, Maj. Gen. William Mahone's division left its position at Bermuda Hundred and moved west toward Goode's Bridge on the Appomattox. The largest column, which crossed the Appomattox at Petersburg and then turned west, included the bulk of Longstreet's First Corps, Gordon's Second Corps,

The six veteran officers pictured here played important roles in the Appomattox Campaign. Four—Maj. Gens. Andrew A. Humphreys, Charles Griffin, Horatio G. Wright, and John G. Parke— served in the Army of the Potomac. The other two—Maj. Gens. John Gibbon and Godfrey Weitzel—were from Ord's Army of the James. Humphreys had been Meade's chief of staff before assuming command of the Second Corps. His men fought gallantly at Sailor's Creek and Cumberland Church. Griffin,

who replaced Gouverneur K. Warren as head of the Fifth Corps after the Battle of Five Forks, helped to block Lee's last attempt to break through the Union lines on April 9. Wright's Sixth Corps helped breach the Petersburg defenses on April 2, forcing the Confederates to abandon that city and Richmond. Four days later they dealt Lee a fatal blow at Sailor's Creek. After helping in the capture of Petersburg, Parke and his Ninth Corps repaired the South Side Railroad for use by Union forces. While part

of Gibbon's Twenty-fourth Corps occupied Richmond, the rest joined in the pursuit of Lee. They fought at High Bridge near Farmville and were the principal troops to engage the Confederates west of Appomattox Court House on April 9. Weitzel's Twenty-fifth Corps was composed entirely of United States Colored Troops. He led one division into Richmond and sent the other under Brig. Gen. William Birney to support the Twenty-fourth Corps.

A. A. Humphreys, 2nd Corps

Charles Griffin, 5th Corps

Horatio G. Wright, 6th Corps

John G. Parke, 9th Corps

John Gibbon, 24th Corps

Godfrey Weitzel, 25th Corps

and Lt. Gen. A. P. Hill's Third Corps (commanded by Longstreet following Hill's death on April 2). Initially ordered to follow a direct route to Bevill's Bridge, Longstreet and Gordon found that crossing flooded and diverted northward to Goode's Bridge. The fourth and southernmost of the columns, commanded by Lt. Gen. Richard H. Anderson, remained south of the Appomattox River. Working west along the river's right bank, Anderson's column included Pickett's division and Fitzhugh Lee's cavalry, just two days removed from their ignominious defeat at Five Forks, as well as Maj. Gen. Bushrod R. Johnson's division. A massive supply train of 1,400 wagons, estimated by one witness to extend for 30 miles, lumbered through the streets of Petersburg as a smaller train of wagons left Richmond beyond the right of Ewell's column. Lee and his headquarters party followed the last of the infantry out of Petersburg, trailing Longstreet's and Gordon's commands.

Grant's plans for the pursuit left Lee with virtually no margin for error. Although the Confederates enjoyed about a half-day's head start, they followed a less direct route. The four southern columns faced marches to the west or northwest before veering south to rendezvous at Amelia Court House and press on toward Burkeville. General Meade suggested that the Federals follow Lee, but Grant replied "that we did not want to follow him; we wanted to get ahead of him and cut him off...." Grant sought to reach a position on the Richmond and Danville Railroad south of Lee's troops, and by marching almost due west, paralleling the Appomattox River beyond Anderson's left flank, the Federals could block the way to North Carolina. Although Grant had not excelled in mathematics at West Point, he certainly grasped the strategic geometry: his armies would follow the base of a triangle defined by Petersburg at one end and Jetersville or Burkeville at the other, while Lee's soldiers would move up to and then away from the triangle's apex at the crossings over the Appomattox River above Amelia Court House. The largest Confederate column, Longstreet's and Gordon's, would trek approximately 55 miles from Petersburg to Burkeville via Goode's Bridge; Federals heading directly for Burkeville from Petersburg would traverse a little more than 36 miles.

The majority of Grant's soldiers took the most

direct route from Petersburg toward Jetersville and Burkeville. Sheridan's cavalry spearheaded the movement, with three infantry corps of the Army of the Potomac—Humphreys's Second, Maj. Gen. Charles Griffin's Fifth, and Maj. Gen. Horatio G. Wright's Sixth—following as closely as possible. (Unhappy with what he considered a lackluster performance, Sheridan had removed Gouverneur Warren from command of the Fifth Corps on the battlefield at Five Forks; Griffin led the corps for the rest of the campaign.) Sheridan possessed a number of unlovely personal characteristics, including a willingness to take credit for the accomplishments of subordinates, but his aggressiveness and undeniable military gifts rendered him the perfect officer to lead a strike force intent on hounding the enemy into submission.

Grant accompanied Ord's Army of the James and Maj. Gen. John G. Parke's Ninth Corps in a second column that marched along the South Side Railroad toward its intersection with the Richmond and Danville Railroad at Burkeville (Parke's command initially trailed the Army of the Potomac before shifting south to join Ord on April 4). The South Side would function as a vital conduit for supplies as the Federals chased Lee, and Grant ordered his lieutenants "to repair the railroad and telegraph as they proceeded." "The road was a 5 foot gauge, while our rolling stock was all of the 4 foot 8½ inch gauge," noted Grant in a passage from his memoirs that attested to his army's engineering and construction prowess, "consequently the rail on one side of the track had to be taken up throughout the whole length and relaid so as to conform to the gauge of our cars and locomotives."

As the armies commenced their marches westward, Grant's troops held decided advantages in numbers and physical condition. More than 112,000 strong (80,000 of whom would be in the principal columns of the pursuit, with the Ninth Corps coming along a bit later), the Federals had suffered few shortages of food or clothing during the winter and spring. Lee's soldiers, in contrast, had subsisted on the leanest of rations for much of the period, and many horses and mules in the Army of Northern Virginia had emerged from the winter in near emaciation. During the second week of March, Lee had warned Secretary of War John C. Breckinridge that

The Appomattox Campaign, April 2-9, 1865

For nine months, from June 1864 to April 1865, armies under Lt. Gen. Ulysses S. Grant besieged Petersburg and Richmond, last strongholds of Gen. Robert E. Lee's soldiers and the Confederate government. Union victory in the Battle of Five Forks on April 1 compelled Lee to evacuate his position to save his army. The next day the Confederates marched away from Petersburg and Richmond and headed west, in-tending to obtain rations at Amelia Court House, then proceed down the railroad to Danville and ultimately join forces with Gen. Joseph E. Johnston's forces in North Carolina.

Warfare became a matter of rapid movements, with Lee retreating and Grant's arm-ies pursuing agressively. (The map below highlights signif-icant aspects of those move-ments.) For the Confederates, disaster piled upon disaster.

At Amelia Court House Lee's hungry and exhausted veter-ans found no rations wait-ing; Union cavalry dashed in upon their wagon trains at every opportunity, while their rear guard was hard pressed by Federal infantry; at Jetersville a strong Union force blocked the retreat south; at Sailor's Creek the Confederate rear guard was cut off and more than 6,000 men were captured; and at Farmville Lee barely beat

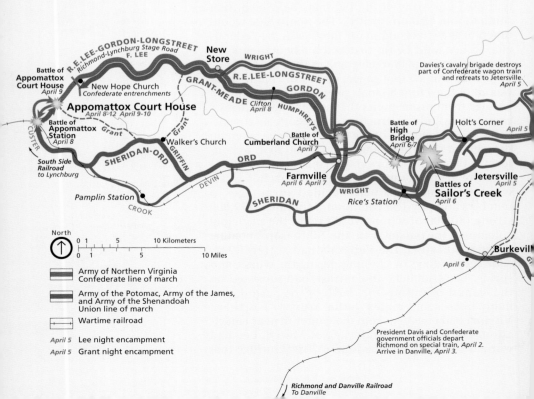

Grant across the Appomattox River, but the race was so close that the main bridge went undestroyed while Grant continued to press hard on Lee's heels. By Saturday night, April 8, in camp just east of Appomattox Court House, Lee realized that his army was trapped.

Most of the roads that the armies of Lee and Grant followed still exist today. In a few places modern, four-lane highways have been built, but to a large degree the narrow, sinuous roads the armies traveled from Petersburg and Richmond to Appomattox Court House are still much as they were then. The farther one gets from Richmond and Petersburg the less the country has changed with the passage of time. Some fields have become forests and some forests have become fields, but by and large the face of the land is similar to that of 1865.

Virginia Civil War Trails has put together a 26-stop driving tour through seven counties connecting Petersburg to Appomattox Court House that follows the route of Lee's retreat. For information about this and other Civil War Trails programs, check at the information desk in the Appomattox Court House Visitor Center or www.civilwartraveler.com on the Internet.

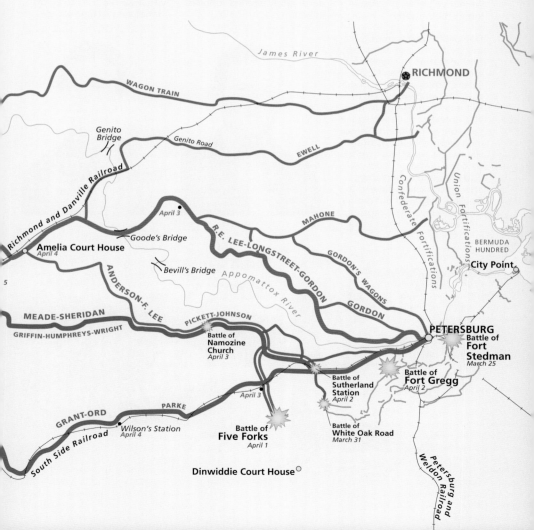

Maj. Gen. Philip Sheridan used the Federal cavalry aggressively throughout the Appomattox Campaign to harass and at times make quick attacks on Lee's weary columns along their line of march. Federal horsemen played critical roles at the battles of Five Forks, Namozine Church, Sailor's Creek, Appomattox Station, and Appomattox Court House. They also destroyed part of a Confederate wagon train near Paineville *(below)* and were involved in the fighting at High Bridge.

One of Sheridan's most effective units was a small group of clandestine horsemen formerly known as the "Jessie Scouts," soldiers who, donning official Confederate uniforms or rustic garb, infiltrated Confederate lines to gain valuable information. These men were now led by Maj. Henry H. Young *(near right)*, a Rhode Islander who was also Sheridan's chief scout and assistant aide-de-camp. On April 3 a squad of Young's scouts deceived and captured

Confederate Brig. Gen. Rufus Barringer and several of his staff as they were looking to rejoin the main Confederate forces after the Battle of Namozine Church. Young's scouts were also responsible for intercepting a dispatch from Lee's commissary general requesting a shipment of supplies be sent to Amelia Court House. This not only gave Sheridan some idea of the size of the Confederate army and its location but the opportunity to capture the desperately needed supplies as well.

Being one of Major Young's scouts was a dangerous occupation, as 20-year-old Archibald H. Rowand Jr. *(shown below in Confederate uniform)* found out on April 7, 1865, when he and a fellow scout were captured, tried, and sentenced to be shot as spies. Rowand managed to escape and his comrade's life was spared when General Lee, possibly feeling the end of the fighting close at hand, declined to authorize the execution. In 1873 Rowand was awarded the Medal of Honor for wartime service.

unless "the men and animals can be subsisted, the army cannot be kept together.... Nor can it be moved to any other position where it can operate to advantage without provisions to enable it to move in a body." Now Lee had undertaken an active campaign that would test the muscle and endurance of men and beasts conditioned to the more sedentary siege warfare of the previous months. Physical privation, disappointment at the loss of Petersburg and Richmond, and the prospect of brutal marching combined to produce a toxic effect on morale and discipline. This was not the supremely confident, highly mobile Confederate army of Second Manassas and Chancellorsville—nor even the veteran instrument that had matched Grant's forces blow for blow in the bloody Overland Campaign of May-June 1864.

Symptoms of a fundamental breakdown surfaced almost as soon as the Confederates left their siege lines. On April 3 a Union soldier at Petersburg described an enemy in crisis: "We didn't get far before we came to one of the roads on which the Rebels fled," he wrote. "They have fallen out all along the line and in the woods, so great in number it seems a literal fulfillment of the oft-repeated phrase, 'the woods are full of them.' One entire regiment, officers and all, surrendered to us as we came along. I noticed a perceptible absence of their usual swagger and none of the enthusiastic expressions of confidence in Lee, which have been so abundant at other times." That same day, a New York sergeant recorded in his diary that 21 Confederates surrendered to him on the banks of the Appomattox River near Petersburg. An anonymous southern signalman's diary illuminated the same phenomenon from a different perspective. Forming to begin their march about midnight on April 2, this man's party had no idea where they were going. "[B]ut we knew this much," he stated bitterly, "it is a retreat. Our gallant and hitherto invincible army of Northern Va. has been overcome by mere brute force of numbers.... [Petersburg & Richmond] are at the tender mercies of a hated but never feared foe."

In his diary entries for April 3-5, Elisha Hunt Rhodes of the 2nd Rhode Island Infantry effectively juxtaposed the high spirits and determination of the Federals against the increasing disorganization of Lee's soldiers. "We heard today that Richmond has

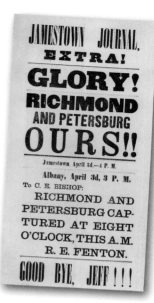

News of the capture of Petersburg and Richmond traveled quickly. This broadside from the Jamestown (N.Y.) Journal *appeared within hours of Federal soldiers occupying the cities. On April 4 President Lincoln visited the Confederate capital, accompanied by his son Tad, Adm. David D. Porter, and a dozen sailors. He called the fall of Richmond the end of a four-year-long nightmare.*

On April 7 the Confederates tried to burn the two bridges over the Appomattox River east of Farmville. The half-mile-long South Side Railroad bridge, known as High Bridge *(above)*, was effectively destroyed, but not the wagon bridge below it. This allowed the Federal Second Corps to continue pursuing the remnants of Lee's army. On April 8 Lee's hopes for obtaining rations for his harried soldiers were dashed completely when the 2nd New York Cavalry captured the Confederate supply trains at Appomattox Station *(below)*, seen here in a photograph taken shortly after the war.

been evacuated and is in flames," he wrote on the 3rd. "Well, let it burn, we do not want it. We are after Lee, and we are going to have him." The next day provided graphic evidence of impending Confederate doom. "Still following the demoralized Army," noted Rhodes. "The road is filled with broken wagons and the things thrown away in the flight of the Rebels. I do not know just where we are but do not care, for Grant is at the head and we shall come out all right." April 5 brought further "proof of the demoralized condition of Lee's troops." Lee "has often followed us, and we him," mused Rhodes, "but this is the last time." Continued pursuit would enable the Federals to catch Lee, "and when we do the war will end."

By the time Rhodes recorded the last of these observations, Lee's original plan for the campaign had been thwarted. The Confederate commander reached Amelia Court House on the morning of April 4, expecting to linger just long enough for his army to come together before pushing on southward. The absence of Ewell's column, which had experienced delays on the Genito Road, forced Lee to wait impatiently as invaluable hours slipped away.

Many accounts have emphasized that Lee also hoped to issue provisions while at Amelia Court House. He found a large cache of ammunition but no rations, and a staff officer recalled that an "anxious and haggard expression came to General Lee's face when he was informed of this great misfortune." That concern likely stemmed more from Ewell's absence, but Lee immediately sent foraging parties into the surrounding countryside. He also issued an appeal to the citizens of Amelia County for any meat, flour, or fodder they could spare. "The Army of Northern Virginia arrived here today, expecting to find plenty of provisions...," he explained in the appeal, "but to my surprise and regret I find not a pound of subsistence for man or horse."

As the empty supply wagons rumbled out in search of food and Lee anxiously awaited Ewell's appearance, Federals pressed relentlessly forward. At about noon, Sheridan sent an optimistic message to army headquarters: "If we press on we will no doubt get the whole army." To that end, the feisty general ordered one of his cavalry divisions and the Fifth Corps to close rapidly on Jetersville while he hastened ahead

"Thank God that I have lived to see this! It seems to me that I have been dreaming a horrid dream for four years, and now the nightmare is gone."

Abraham Lincoln, April 3, 1865, after learning of the Federal occupation of Richmond and Petersburg and the pursuit of Lee

> *"Tired and hungry we push on. It is now a race for life or death. We seldom receive orders now."*
>
> William M. Owen, Washington Artillery of New Orleans, Army of Northern Virginia, C.S.A., April 5, 1865

with his personal escort—200 troopers of the First United States Cavalry—and took up a preliminary defensive position near that village. Shortly after reaching Jetersville, Sheridan's party captured a Confederate courier who carried a document posted from Lee's commissary general at Amelia Court House asking that 300,000 rations be shipped from Danville and Lynchburg to Burkeville. "There was thus revealed not only the important fact that Lee was concentrating at Amelia Court House," Sheridan later observed, "but also a trustworthy basis for estimating his troops...." Rapid action would deny Lee a direct route to Burkeville. By late afternoon on April 4, some of Griffin's Fifth Corps Union infantry had arrived at Jetersville and begun to erect substantial works. The swing of picks and thrust of shovels at Jetersville helped set the stage for a decisive confrontation.

Lee awoke on a damp Wednesday, April 5, that would bring nothing but discouraging news for the retreating Confederates. He prodded his tired and hungry soldiers south toward Burkeville, expecting to confront only Federal cavalry along the Richmond and Danville Railroad and believing his infantry could clear them away. But the Confederates soon encountered Sheridan's strong position at Jetersville. Reports that additional Union infantry was approaching aggravated an already critical situation. As firing sputtered along the lines shortly after 1 p.m., Lee conducted a personal reconnaissance with Longstreet and some other officers. His instinct told him to break through the Union blocking force. "I never saw Gen. Lee seem so anxious to bring on a battle in my life," recalled Porter Alexander, who noted that a full realization of the odds Lee faced "seemed to disappoint him greatly." The loss of time at Amelia Court House had been fatal. Soon Humphreys's Second Corps and Wright's Sixth Corps, ordered on the evening of April 4 to support Sheridan, would buttress the Federal line at Jetersville. The planned route to Burkeville, and thence to North Carolina, had been denied Lee.

Jetersville marked the defining moment of the campaign. Under a sullen sky that mirrored spirits in the Army of Northern Virginia, Lee abandoned his effort to escape southward and determined instead to march west toward Farmville. He hoped to get beyond the grasping reach of the Federals to a point on the South Side Railroad where he could draw supplies from Lynchburg. If successful, he could feed his army and try again to turn south toward Danville. Lee ordered a forced march on the night of April 5-6 in an effort to put some distance between his army and the Federals. Men and animals driven to the edge of their capacity strained through the blackness, enduring innumerable halts and starts along poor roads and at stream crossings. The supply train, part of which had fallen victim to Federal cavalry, remained north of the army's main body and experienced an especially hellish night. Lee's principal column now stretched out for more than 15 miles along a single road. As Confederates groped their way west from Amelia Court House and Jetersville, Lee received a captured telegram from Grant to Ord, dated 10:10 p.m. on April 5, that placed the Army of the James at Burkeville and the Army of the Potomac at Jetersville. However many miles the Confederates might cover on their night march, Lee knew that virtually all of the Federal forces would remain within easy reach.

Grant met with Meade and Sheridan about midnight on April 5 to discuss how best to get at their reeling enemy. Beginning the day with Ord's army along the South Side Railroad, Grant had received information from Sheridan about the position and condition of the Confederate army that pointed to "a life and death struggle with Lee to get south to his provisions." At Sheridan's suggestion, he decided to ride across country to join the Army of the Potomac. Meade had concluded about mid-afternoon that Lee would dig in around Amelia Court House, and he advocated a carefully prepared advance against that point. Sheridan countered that Lee seemed to be moving off to the west and should be harried as much as possible. Shortly after 10 p.m., Grant reached Sheridan's headquarters and soon heard his lieutenant argue that Meade's plan to advance deliberately against Amelia Court House would allow Lee to distance himself from the Federals. The pair then rode to the Army of the Potomac's headquarters at the Childress House, where Grant explained to Meade "that we did not want to follow the enemy; we wanted to get ahead of him." The Federal infantry at Jetersville would march to Amelia Court House at 6

"General Lee was riding everywhere... encouraging his...men by his calm and cheerful bearing."

John B. Gordon, major general, Second Corps, Army of Northern Virginia, C.S.A.

Richard S. Ewell was a corps commander before an injury made him unfit for field command. Known to his troops as "Old Bald Head," he was in charge of the defenses of Richmond above James River until April 2, 1865.

William Mahone was one of Lee's most trusted officers and, from the Wilderness to Appomattox, one of the most effective divisional commanders of either side. The men of his division called him "Skin and Bones" Mahone.

a.m. the next morning, then swing around to pursue Lee. Sheridan's horsemen, meanwhile, would move west on a line parallel and a bit south of the Confederates. Ord would continue his progress along the South Side Railroad.

Well before mid-morning on April 6, a day of sporadically heavy rains, the Federals advancing on Amelia Court House perceived that Lee's army lay to the west. Humphreys's and Griffin's corps marched in that direction, while Wright's corps dropped in behind the cavalry. Wright's Sixth Corps, along with units of the Nineteenth Corps and a pair of mounted divisions had fought as part of Sheridan's Army of the Shenandoah during the 1864 Shenandoah Valley campaign, and Grant hoped the infantry and cavalry would add to their sterling record of cooperative success. The Sixth Corps remained attached to Sheridan's command through April 9, though Grant had returned the Fifth Corps to Meade on the 5th.

The Army of Northern Virginia endured one of its darkest days on April 6. Proceeding southwestward on a line roughly parallel to the Richmond and Danville Railroad, Lee expected to gather his army at Rice's Station, a point on the South Side Railroad a few miles west of Burkeville. The infantry of the First Corps and the Third Corps under Longstreet began arriving that morning, soon followed by Mahone's division. But Anderson's column, which included Pickett's division and should have been next in line, failed to appear, as did Ewell's command and Gordon's Second Corps. A worried Lee rode to a piece of high ground overlooking the watershed of Sailor's Creek, a lazy tributary of the Appomattox River, to find out why the rest of this army had lagged behind.

Before Lee reached his vantage point above Sailor's Creek, pursuing Federals had wreaked havoc among the commands of Anderson, Ewell, and Gordon. Federal cavalry had harassed the flanks of the southern columns throughout the day, and Union infantry had compelled the Confederates to deploy again and again to beat back small-scale, nagging attacks along a succession of hills and in shallow valleys. A Massachusetts soldier described making contact with Gordon's infantry, which brought up the Confederate rear, and then "keeping up a running fight and a brisk skirmishing" along a road "strewn with tents, camp equipage, battery forges, limbers [for pulling

The Civil War was fought before photographers were able to capture motion successfully, and pictorial representations of battles and armies on the march came from newspaper engravings based on battlefield sketches supplied by "special artists" accompanying the armies. One of the most prominent of these "specials" was Alfred R. Waud of *Harper's Weekly* and the only newspaper artist accompanying the Union armies in the pursuit of Lee. He witnessed and sketched the surrender of Lt. Gen. Richard S. Ewell's corps at Little Sailor's Creek on April 6 *(top)*. He called that event "quite an effective incident," with "the soldiers silhouetted against the western sky... their muskets thrown butt upwards in token of surrender as our troops closed in...." Waud also caught Brig. Gen. George A. Custer preparing his troopers for another charge against Lt. Gen. Richard H. Anderson's division *(bottom)*. It was the routing of Anderson's troops that led to Ewell's surrender. Neither of these drawings appeared in *Harper's Weekly* because of the extensive coverage the newspaper accorded Lincoln's assassination on April 14 and the long funeral that followed.

cannon], wagons" abandoned by the hard-pressed enemy.

At Holt's Corner, a crossroads about six miles northeast of Rice's Station, the trailing elements of Lee's army divided. Anderson deployed his command to ward off Federal cavalry, a maneuver that created a gap between him and Longstreet's units. Anderson eventually resumed his march, followed by Ewell's troops, crossing Little Sailor's Creek and ascending high ground en route to Rice's Station. The army's wagon train and Gordon's corps took a different route from Holt's Corner, keeping Little Sailor's Creek to their left as they proceeded northwest toward other roads that would take them to Rice's Station.

Federals soon closed in on both groups of Confederates. Sheridan's cavalry blocked Anderson's advance, exerting pressure from the south and southeast and employing the superior firepower of their repeating weapons, while Wright's Sixth Corps artillery and infantry hammered Ewell's bedraggled troops, who lacked artillery and had taken up a defensive line on the high west bank of Little Sailor's Creek. Off to the north, Humphreys's Second Corps forced the supply trains and Gordon's corps into jumbled disorder along the soggy banks of Sailor's Creek. The action intensified between about 5:15 and 6:30 p.m. Gordon subsequently wrote about how the Federals "struck my command while we were endeavoring to push the ponderous wagon trains through the bog, out of which the starved teams were unable to drag them." Anderson's line collapsed first, followed by Ewell's, and thousands of Confederates streamed away from the action. Of approximately 11,600 who fought along Little Sailor's Creek, at least 6,000 were killed, wounded, or captured. Gordon lost 2,000 men and nearly 300 wagons and ambulances before reaching safety on the high western bank of Sailor's Creek. Among those taken prisoner were eight Confederate generals, including Ewell, who had made his reputation under Stonewall Jackson during the glory days of 1862, and Maj. Gen. George Washington Custis Lee, the commanding general's oldest son, who led troops in the field for the first time during the retreat from Richmond.

Dusk drew near as Robert E. Lee witnessed the final stage of this panorama of disaster. Ordering

Mahone's division to help cover the withdrawal of Anderson's and Ewell's battered units, Lee manifested considerable distress. Mahone recalled that Lee straightened himself in the saddle and muttered, more to himself than to anyone else, "My God! has the army been dissolved?" Sgt. John H. Carter of the 1st Massachusetts Heavy Artillery told the Union side of the story in a single telling sentence: "It was a beautiful day, and it had been full of intense excitement and glorious results." Philip Sheridan drew new energy from the overwhelming victory. Near midnight, he sent Grant a dispatch that closed with a confident call for action: "If the thing is pressed I think Lee will surrender." Grant passed the message along to Lincoln, who for the first three years of the war had tried vainly to find generals with Sheridan's determination to smite the rebels. Quoting Sheridan's message, Lincoln replied simply at 11 a.m. on April 7: "Let the thing be pressed."

The debacle at Sailor's Creek focused Lee's thoughts on how to gain some distance on Grant's pursuing armies. Although he knew that hunger and bone-weariness stalked his soldiers, he ordered the campaign's third night march. He hoped to beat the Federals to Farmville, muster his army north of the Appomattox River, and, having destroyed readily available bridges, leave Grant's armies stranded south of the Appomattox. Thus liberated from direct pressure, reasoned Lee, the Army of Northern Virginia would continue to march westward in an attempt to get around the Federal forces and head south to unite with Johnston's army. The Confederates left Sailor's Creek in two main columns. Longstreet's units stayed south of the Appomattox on the shortest route to Farmville, while Gordon and Mahone angled northwest along the South Side Railroad to its crossing over the Appomattox at High Bridge (an imposing structure nearly 2,500 feet long and 126 feet high, built in 1854, that dwarfed a modest wagon bridge running alongside it). The army hemorrhaged badly as the columns crawled along muddy, badly rutted roads. "[M]en and horses were utterly worn down by fatigue, loss of sleep and hunger," wrote one Confederate. "Thousands were leaving their commands and wandering about the devastated country in quest of food, and they had no muskets." Porter Alexander noted that it took him eight hours to cover

Edward Porter Alexander, Longstreet's chief of artillery, had fought in nearly all the major battles of the Eastern Theater of war, from First Manassas to the Appomattox Campaign, and was considered the Confederacy's most prominent artillerist. Joseph E. Johnston wanted him to become chief of artillery in the Army of Tennessee. Lee refused to let him go.

African Americans in the Appomattox Campaign

While most of the regiments of United States Colored Troops were involved in the occupation of Richmond and Petersburg on April 3 and after, seven regiments (approximately 2,000 men or three percent of the Federal force) accompanied Maj. Gen. Edward O. C. Ord's Army of the James to Appomattox Court House and arrived in time to be involved in the final fighting. These units were all from Gen. William Birney's division and included the 8th, 29th, 31st, 41st, 45th, 116th, and 127th U.S.C.T. The 29th, 31st, and 116th U.S.C.T. participated in the advance on the Confederate line in the closing phase of the Battle of Appomattox Court House on the morning of April 9.

African Americans also accompanied Lee's army. Desperate for manpower, the Confederate government had on March 23, 1865, issued General Order No. 14 allowing for the enlistment of blacks into Confederate service. This was too late to have much effect, but the recruit-ment effort did bear fruit in Richmond, where two or three companies were formed and, according to the Richmond *Daily Examiner*, displayed a remarkable "knowledge of the military art." These soldiers joined Custis Lee's wagon train after Richmond was evacuated. Blacks also provided yeoman service to the First Regiment Engineer Troops mounding roads, repairing bridges, and cutting new roads when old ones became impassable.

The only documented example of "official" black troops serving the Confederacy in Virginia as a unit under fire comes from a Union chaplain who observed "many negroes recently armed by Jef. Davis" among Confederates captured at Sailor's Creek. When Lee surrendered at Appomattox, 36 African Americans were listed on the Confederate paroles. Most were servants, free blacks, musicians, cooks, teamsters, or blacksmiths.

There are no known photographs of the U.S.C.T. regiments that took part in the Appomattox campaign. The unit shown below is the 29th Connecticut and is typical in appearance of other U.S.C.T. regiments. Two companies from this regiment were the first Union infantry to enter Richmond after its evacuation. The inset shows black teamsters in the Army of the James.

Richard H. Anderson was one of the best brigade and division commanders in the Confederate army but performed poorly at corps level. "He was a very brave man, but of a rather inert, indolent manner for commanding troops in the field, and by no means pushing or aggressive," one of his adjutants wrote. After his corps was shattered at Little Sailor's Creek, Lee relieved him of command and divided his remaining divisions between Longstreet and Gordon.

six miles during a night that he termed "actively wretched."

On Friday morning, April 7, Longstreet's units reached Farmville, a town of 1,500 situated on the right bank of the Appomattox River. Under a steady rain that would soak the countryside throughout the day, the Confederates crossed to the north side of the river via a pair of bridges (one of which bore the tracks of the South Side Railroad). The famished men received regular rations—the first since April 2 for many of them—that had been shipped to Farmville from Burkeville as Ord's Army of the James approached. Before the men could cook their food, Lee learned that Federals had gained control of the wagon bridge below High Bridge. His temper flared briefly, after which he summoned Porter Alexander, pulled out a map, and discussed the positions of the armies. Alexander eagerly looked at the map, only to discover that "the most direct & shortest road" westward toward Appomattox Court House from Farmville "did not cross the river as we had done, but kept up the south side near the railroad." Lee's gamble that the inside track to Appomattox Court House held less advantage than the prospect of placing the Appomattox River between himself and the enemy had failed. He instructed Alexander to oversee burning the two bridges at Farmville and, with Federal cavalry skirmishing with some of Fitzhugh Lee's Confederate troopers just outside the town, ordered Longstreet's men to march north about two and one-half miles.

Rapid Federal movements had ensured the failure of Lee's plan to place the Appomattox River between himself and Grant. Humphreys's Second Corps followed its success at Sailor's Creek with a diligent pursuit of Gordon and Mahone. The Confederates attempted to burn both the High Bridge and the modest wagon span when they crossed early in the morning, but Humphreys's first troops arrived by 7 a.m. and extinguished the flames. Union engineers rapidly repaired the damage to the wagon bridge, allowing Humphreys to renew the chase by mid-morning. On the south side of the Appomattox, Maj. Gen. George H. Crook's cavalry division, Ord's Army of the James, and Wright's Sixth Corps maintained pressure on Longstreet (the first of them arriving at Farmville before noon), and other Federal cavalry took position to prevent Lee's making a dash for Danville. By late afternoon, Ord's army and Wright's corps stood massed in Farmville. Some Federal cavalry crossed the Appomattox at a nearby ford, menacing the Confederate supply trains before being driven off.

The most serious fighting on April 7 occurred late in the afternoon near Cumberland Church. Gordon and Mahone reached the church, not quite three miles north of Farmville, early in the afternoon. They skirmished with Humphreys's advancing units and then, supported by some of Longstreet's troops, repelled heavier attacks after 4 p.m. Nearly 600 Federals and an undetermined number of Confederates fell in the action, which ended with Lee in a precarious position. He had uttered the first known allusion to the subject of surrender in a comment to his son William Henry Fitzhugh that afternoon. Known as "Rooney" and a major general of cavalry, Lee's son had helped Col. T. T. Munford's and Maj. Gen. Thomas Rosser's divisions repel the Union cavalry foray against the Confederate supply trains. "Keep your command together and in good spirits, General," Lee told Rooney in words that likely reflected at least a touch of bravado, "don't let them think of surrender—I will get you out of this."

Grant established his headquarters at the Randolph House (also known as the Prince Edward Hotel) in Farmville on the afternoon of April 7. By then, he knew how severely he had circumscribed Lee's options. He had seen ample signs of eroding morale among Lee's soldiers. The Federals had scooped up thousands of prisoners, stragglers infested the countryside, and weary Confederates had cast aside enormous amounts of arms and equipment. The time seemed propitious, believed Grant, to propose an end to hostilities. At 5 p.m., he composed a two-sentence note to Lee: "The results of the last week must convince you of the hopelessness of further resistance on the part of the Army of Northern Va. in this struggle. I feel that it is so and regard it as my duty to shift from myself the responsibility of any further effusion of blood by asking of you the surrender of that portion of the C. S. army known as the Army of Northern Va." Brig. Gen. Seth Williams, Grant's adjutant general, carried the note through Confederate lines.

> *"General Lee's forces were now reduced to... minimum strength, but a fiercer, more determined body of men never lived."*
>
> Herman H. Perry, captain, Sorrel's Brigade, Army of Northern Virginia, C.S.A., following the Battle of Sailor's Creek

> *"If there is any hope for the Confederacy it is in delay. For if the Army of Northern Va. surrenders every other army will surrender as fast as the news reaches it. For it is the morale of this army that has supported the whole Confederacy."*
>
> Edward Porter Alexander, brigadier general, First Corps artillery, Army of Northern Virginia, C.S.A., April 9, 1865

Lee received the communication between 9:30 and 10 p.m. James Longstreet sat close by as his impassive chief evaluated Grant's proposal, then handed it to him. Longstreet read it and returned it to Lee with a simple response: "Not yet." Lee's answer to Grant, which he did not discuss with Longstreet, opened the door for further communication: "Though not entertaining the opinion you express of the hopelessness of further resistance on the part of the Army of N. Va.—I reciprocate your desire to avoid useless effusion of blood, & therefore before considering your proposition, ask the terms you will offer on condition of its surrender." The message soon reached Brig. Gen. Seth Williams, a friend of Lee's from the pre-war army, who delivered it to Grant early in the morning on April 8.

Grant wrote a second note to Lee as he prepared Union forces for another day's pursuit. He ignored Lee's denial that the Confederacy's war had reached a hopeless point, replying instead to the question about terms: "I would say that peace being my great desire there is but one condition I insist upon, namely: that the men and officers surrendered shall be disqualified for taking up arms again, against the Government of the United States, until properly exchanged. I will meet you or will designate Officers to meet any officers you may name for the same purpose, at any point agreeable to you, for the purpose of arranging definitely the terms upon which the surrender of the Army of N. Va. will be received." Having presented Lee with a second chance to stop the fighting, Grant dispatched the note and then rode across the Appomattox to catch up with the Second and Sixth corps (the latter having crossed the river during the night), which were moving in the tracks of Lee's army. Below the Appomattox, Sheridan's cavalry, the Army of the James, and the Fifth Corps moved westward along the South Side Railroad.

Sheridan dominated the Union effort on April 8. No other Union officer matched his zeal. Grant's memoirs speak glowingly about how Sheridan's "troops moved with alacrity and without any straggling." They anticipated the end of four years' struggle, and "[n]othing seemed to fatigue them. They were ready to move without rations and travel without rest until the end." Grant also praised the foot soldiers—thousands of them African Americans in

Ord's army—who toiled in the wake of Sheridan's troopers, observing that they "marched about as rapidly as the cavalry could." Cavalry divisions under Maj. Gen. George A. Custer, Maj. Gen. George Crook, and Brig. Gen. Thomas C. Devin (all from Merritt's command) operated in the vanguard, pounding toward Appomattox Station and Pamplin Station respectively. Sheridan had learned that Confederate supplies awaited Lee at Appomattox Station, and he meant to bend every effort to get there ahead of Lee's fleeing army. Grant proved unable to participate fully in the exhilarating Union pursuit because of the onset of crippling migraine headaches. He covered just 10 miles by mid-afternoon and went to bed at Clifton, a house on the Richmond-Lynchburg Stage Road where he hoped to find rest that would quell the pain.

This battle flag of the 61st Virginia Volunteer Infantry, a regiment in Maj. Gen. William Mahone's division, was carried through all of the major campaigns from Fredericksburg until the end of the war. It was surrendered at Appomattox Court House on April 9, 1865, and carried home by a Connecticut officer. The flag was presented to the National Park Service in 1953 by the widow of Pulitzer Prize-winning historian Douglas Southall Freeman, whose father had served in the unit.

Lee's headaches were of a different sort. His army left the vicinity of Cumberland Church on the night of April 7-8, taking various routes that converged at a hamlet on the Richmond-Lynchburg Stage Road called New Store. The stage road ran northwest from New Store before angling sharply southwest to Appomattox Station on the South Side Railroad—a distance of about 20 miles. Sheridan's Federals south of the Appomattox River followed a much shorter and more direct route along the South Side. Not only distance but also physical condition increasingly favored the Federals. "Many of the men, from exhaustion, were lying prone upon the ground, only waiting for the enemy to come and pick them up," wrote a Confederate of the march on April 8, "while at intervals horses and mules lying in the mud had struggled to extricate themselves until exhaustion had forced them to be still and wait for death to glaze their wildly staring eyes."

The stalwart elements of Lee's army continued their march past New Store. Gordon's corps took the lead, with Longstreet's command next and Fitzhugh Lee's cavalry guarding the rear. The rains of the previous day mercifully had stopped. Although Federals lurked not far behind, they provoked little skirmishing. Porter Alexander termed it the first "quiet day of the march, since leaving Amelia." During the morning, Brig. Gen. William Nelson Pendleton, the army's chief of artillery, reported to Lee that several officers had met the previous evening and concluded the mo-

ment had come to ask Grant for terms. They hoped
that by raising the issue themselves Lee would be
spared the dishonor of broaching the topic with
Grant. Lee firmly rejected the overture with an affir-
mation that too many gallant men remained in the
ranks to justify such a move. That afternoon, because
they no longer had sufficient troops to command, he
relieved Richard H. Anderson, George E. Pickett,
and Bushrod R. Johnson from their responsibilities
with the army, assigning the post-Sailor's Creek remnants of their commands to Gordon and Longstreet.
Only Anderson seems to have taken Lee's action in
stride; Pickett, already aggrieved because of the failed
attack by his division on the third day at Gettysburg,
nursed a deep animosity toward Lee. Both Johnson
and Pickett continued on, however, and were paroled
with the army at Appomattox Court House.

Either late in the afternoon or sometime after dark,
Grant's second message caught up with Lee, who
pondered its contents before asking Lt. Col. Charles
Venable of his staff how he would respond. Venable
replied that he would ignore Grant's communication. "Ah, but it must be answered," said Lee. He
then composed a note that somewhat incongruously
expressed a desire to end the fighting without surrendering the Army of Northern Virginia. "To be
frank," it read in part, "I do not think the emergency
has arisen to call for the surrender of this Army, but
as the restoration of peace should be the sole object
of all, I desired to know whether your proposals
would lead to that and I cannot therefore meet you
with a view to surrender the Army of N. Va.—but as
far as your proposal may affect the C.S. forces under
my command & tend to the restoration of peace, I
shall be pleased to meet you at 10 a.m. tomorrow on
the old stage road to Richmond between the picket
lines of the two armies." The message soon was on its
way to A. A. Humphreys's Federal lines. That evening the Confederates bivouacked in camps that
spread out for several miles along the stage road,
with the most advanced units, of Longstreet's and
Gordon's commands, extending into the eastern
edge of the town of Appomattox Court House and
two or three miles beyond New Hope Church.

Lee convened his last council of war that night.
The site has not been established beyond doubt.
Substantial evidence places it east of the Richmond-

Lynchburg Stage Road overlooking Rocky Run, where Lee made his headquarters, but other accounts suggest it was several miles farther back near Longstreet's rearguard. Under a chilly, moonlit sky, Longstreet, Gordon, and Fitzhugh Lee joined their commander around a warming campfire. Lee informed them of his exchange of notes with Grant. They knew Federals blocked the road beyond Appomattox but lacked specific information about the enemy's composition and strength. If it were only cavalry ahead of them, the Army of Northern Virginia might be able to break through. They agreed that Fitzhugh Lee's troopers would attack in the early hours of Sunday, April 9, supported by Gordon. If they managed to clear the road, the army would resume its retreat. Should the Federals prove too strong, surrender stood as the only option.

From their positions southwest, south, and east of Lee's army on the night of April 8, Grant's soldiers could review a handsome day's work. Sheridan's indefatigable cavalry had swept along the South Side Railroad. Crook's troopers had seized a significant amount of Confederate materiel at Pamplin Station around 11 a.m., and Wesley Merritt's command, with the colorful and impetuous George Armstrong Custer in the van, had descended on Appomattox Station late in the afternoon, capturing several trains and skirmishing with Confederates in the direction of Appomattox Court House. Custer also captured 25 pieces of artillery and took almost a thousand prisoners. The last firing, echoes of which probably reached Lee's headquarters, died away after 9 p.m. Sheridan rode onto the scene about the same time, sized up the situation, and sent one of Crook's brigades to block Lee's route west. He also sent orders for Ord to hurry his infantry forward to join the cavalry at Appomattox Station. Anticipating a move of the type Lee and his council of war planned later that night, Sheridan shared his thoughts with Grant. "I do not think Lee means to surrender until compelled to do so," he stated, but if Ord's infantry arrived the Federals could "finish the job" on April 9.

Grant's headache continued throughout the evening and into the next day. Near midnight, a courier arrived at Clifton with Lee's latest message. Its tone struck Brig. Gen. John A. Rawlins, Grant's chief of staff, as similar to that in Lee's early-March proposal

"If General Lee doesn't know when to surrender until I tell him, he will never know."

James Longstreet, lieutenant general, First Corps, Army of Northern Virginia, C.S.A., April 8, 1865

for a military convention. Lincoln had left no doubt that only he could address larger questions of ending the war, and Rawlins heatedly complained that Lee sought "to arrange for peace—something beyond and above the surrender of his army—something to embrace the whole Confederacy, if possible." More measured in his reaction, Grant believed he and Lee could "settle the whole business in an hour" if only they could meet. He answered Lee early Sunday morning, stating plainly that he lacked authority to "treat on the subject of peace." "The terms upon which peace can be had are well understood," he added. "By the South laying down their Arms they will hasten that most desirable event, save thousands of human lives and hundreds of Millions of property not yet destroyed." Perhaps sensing that the decisive action would transpire "at the head of the column," Grant set out on a long ride to join Sheridan that would take him south and then west and consume several hours.

Military events sped toward a dramatic conclusion while Grant's party remained out of touch with either wing of the Federal army. Gordon and Fitzhugh Lee formed their units in the pre-dawn darkness, with Gordon's infantry astride Tibb's Lane just west of the village of Appomattox Court House and Lee's troopers on their right. They advanced at dawn, partly shrouded by fog, and soon made headway against Sheridan's troopers. But upon reaching a ridge west of the village they confronted masses of Union infantry. Ord's redoubtable veterans had marched 30 miles in the last 24 hours (a brigade of black soldiers in Brig. Gen. William Birney's division had covered 96 miles in three and a half days), with Griffin's Fifth Corps units matching their killing pace. As these men filed into position, Confederate hopes to break free of the encircling Union host evaporated. Fitzhugh Lee and 1,500 to 2,000 of his troopers soon disengaged from the fighting and rode toward Lynchburg. Gordon had sent word earlier to Robert E. Lee that his corps had been fought "to a frazzle" and could do no more without support from Longstreet.

Lee knew that Longstreet's men had their hands full with the Union Second and Sixth Corps at New Hope Church. Earlier in the morning he had gently chastised Porter Alexander for suggesting that the Army of Northern Virginia should disband and scat-

While Lee was arranging to contact Grant for a meeting "to deal with the question of the surrender of my army," he asked Longstreet to tell General Gordon to cease firing and arrange a truce to avoid unnecessary casualties. One of the riders Gordon sent to carry a white flag and message to General Sheridan to suspend fighting until Lee and Grant had completed their meeting was a member of Longstreet's staff, Capt. Robert M. Sims *(shown right in a postwar photograph)*. The "flag" Sims carried, which he was asked to conceal until well beyond the Confederate lines to prevent the soldiers from becoming demoralized, was really a brand new towel *(part of which is shown here)* that Sims had purchased in Richmond shortly before the city was evacuated.

Sims was unable to locate Sheridan but Lt. Col. Edward W. Whitaker of the 7th Michigan Cavalry took him to his regiment's commander, Maj. Gen. George A. Custer. A sketch of that meeting *(above)* was made by *Har-per's Weekly* artist Alfred R. Waud. Custer sent Whitaker and another staff officer back with Sims to demand an unconditional surrender, which Longstreet promptly refused. A suspension of hostilities was subsequently arranged with Sheridan.

Colonel Whitaker, seeking a souvenir, asked Sims to give him the towel he had used as a truce flag. "I'll see you in hell first!" the captain exploded. "It is humiliating enough to have had to carry it and exhibit it; I'm not going to let you preserve it as a monument to our defeat."

Cutting up the tree under which Grant & Lee met. for Harper's — A.R.W.

When Lt. Col. Orville Babcock came into Confederate lines to arrange a meeting between Lee and Grant, Lee was sitting against a tree in the Sweeney apple orchard a short distance northeast of the village of Appomattox Court House. After word spread that the Army of Northern Virginia had been surrendered, soldiers who had seen the two men talking mistook Babcock for Grant and assumed the surrender had taken place under the apple tree. Wanting souvenirs of the event, both Union and Confederate soldiers cut pieces from the tree until nothing remained, not even the roots. Alfred R. Waud sketched the scene for Harper's Weekly.

ter rather than surrender to Grant. Such a course would prolong the conflict, Lee stated, the "country would be full of lawless bands in every part, & a state of society would ensue from which it would take the country years to recover." Gordon's pessimistic message illuminated the harsh truth. If the Second Corps had failed, Lee remarked to no one in particular, "Then there is nothing left me to do but to go and see General Grant, and I would rather die a thousand deaths."

Lee rode toward the Federal position on Longstreet's end of the line, where he expected to find Grant for the 10 a.m. meeting he had proposed the previous day. He found instead, under a flag of truce, Lt. Col. Charles A. Whittier of Humphreys's staff, who gave him Grant's message written that morning. Lee asked Lt. Col. Charles Marshall of his staff to draft a reply requesting an interview to discuss surrender of the army. A second message to Grant soon followed, asking for a suspension of hostilities pending the results of the interview. General Meade, in charge of the Federals in Longstreet's front and unable to communicate with Grant, subsequently suggested that a duplicate of Lee's first note might reach Grant more quickly at some other point. Lee sent such a note, his third to Grant that day, through Sheridan's lines. He also instructed Gordon to raise flags of truce.

As the sun climbed toward noon, having vanquished the morning's fog to preside over a bright spring day, Gordon's and a portion of Longstreet's troops formed along a ridge north of the Appomattox River. Porter Alexander placed a row of artillery pieces to support them. Lee sought a brief rest under an apple tree on the east side of the stage road a few hundred yards north of the river. Meade and Ord agreed to temporary cease-fires on the eastern and western ends of the field, after which they, like Lee, awaited Grant's response. A few officers from each side, including Longstreet and Ord, drifted into the village, which in April 1865 consisted of about three dozen structures large and small and claimed just more than 50 inhabitants. The men gathered in front of the two-story brick courthouse and conversed for about an hour. "[P]rominent officers...who had not met, except in battle, for four years," recalled Union Maj. Gen. John Gibbon, "mingled together and chatted. All wore an air of anxiety, but all seemed hopeful that there would be no further necessity for bloodshed."

A Union messenger carrying Lee's initial note of the 9th eventually found Grant on the road from Walker's Church to Appomattox Court House. "When the officer reached me," Grant wrote later with a touch of humor, "I was still suffering with the sick headache; but the instant I saw the contents of the note I was cured." The punctilious Rawlins pronounced Lee's message acceptable, and Grant dictated a brief reply dated 11:50 a.m., giving his position and assuring Lee that he would "push forward to the front for the purpose of meeting you." Lt. Col. Orville E. Babcock, an aide-de-camp on Grant's staff, spurred off to give the note to Lee, leaving the general's party to follow at a less urgent gait.

Babcock delivered the message before 1 p.m. James Longstreet was with Lee when Babcock and his Confederate escort drew near the impromptu army headquarters at Sweeney's small apple orchard. "General," said the corps commander who had been Lee's senior lieutenant for virtually the entire war, "unless he offers us honorable terms, come back and let us fight it out." Lee read the message, approved of its content, and steeled himself for the most painful act in the historic drama of the past nine days. Although Grant earlier had offered to allow subordinates to

"All feeling of animosity was forgotten in the tide of joyous victory that swept through the ranks. Everyone knew that the end of hard marches and severe fighting was at hand...."

D. Craft, chaplain, 141st Pennsylvania Volunteers, Army of the Potomac, U.S.A., April 9, 1865

prepare the details of surrender, Lee would shoulder the responsibility himself. Perhaps, as Charles Marshall of his staff later suggested, he had in mind his father's comments about British commander Lord Cornwallis at Yorktown. "Light Horse Harry" Lee had expressed admiration for Cornwallis's generalship but deprecated his decision to send a stand-in to the surrender ceremony: "The British general in this instance," wrote the elder Lee tartly in his memoir, "deviated from his usual line of conduct, dimming the splendor of his long and brilliant career."

Lee instructed Marshall to locate a house suitable for the meeting. A short search led to the home of Wilmer McLean, who, in one of history's small ironies, had owned a farm near the battlefields of First and Second Manassas before moving to Appomattox. McLean's house was a substantial brick structure, three stories high with a columned porch across the front, that stood a short distance west of the courthouse on the south side of the Richmond-Lynchburg Stage Road. Lee and Babcock soon made their way through the village to the house, and Lee climbed the front steps, entered the hall, and turned left into a parlor with furnishings that included several chairs, at least two tables, a sofa, and a large secretary. Lee seated himself, and, along with Babcock and Marshall, waited for Grant.

The Federal commander met Sheridan and Ord at the outskirts of the village about 1:30 p.m. Grant exchanged greetings with his cavalry chief, who informed him that Lee was in the village. "Come, let us go over," Grant said to Sheridan and Ord, and a small cavalcade of Federals clattered toward McLean's house. A number of blue-clad officers soon followed Grant into the parlor—among them Sheridan, Ord, and Capt. Robert Todd Lincoln, the President's son and a junior member of Grant's staff. Notably absent was General Meade, who had commanded the Army of the Potomac for nearly half the war. Although Meade's partisans later accused Grant of a deliberate snub, events simply moved too quickly to allow Meade to participate in the ceremony. He was beyond Lee's army to the northeast, and Grant likely wished to spare Lee an excruciating wait while Meade rode to the village.

Sheridan penned a memorable description of the two great antagonists in McLean's parlor. "General

The McLeans of Appomattox Court House

When Col. Charles Marshall selected the place for the meeting between Lee and Grant, he chose the most impressive home in the village of Appomattox Court House —a large three-story brick house that sat back from the Richmond-Lynchburg Stage Road not far from the courthouse. In the rear were a kitchen, quarters for slaves, a garden, and a barn.

The house's owner, Wilmer McLean *(left)*, was a short, stout man of 50, who had been born and grew up in Alexandria, Virginia (then part of the District of Columbia). As a young man, he worked in a wholesale grocery firm, gaining valuable knowledge of the business world and making important contacts among importers, merchants, and bankers. In 1853 he married Virginia Mason, a wealthy widow with three daughters and extensive real estate holdings that included "Yorkshire," an estate in Prince William County where the McLeans decided to live.

After the Civil War began McLean rented "Yorkshire" to the Confederate army and moved his family to a place of safety. In July 1861 the estate became part of the First Manassas battlefield. By the time a second battle was

fought in the same area a year later, McLean had become a merchant-trader who speculated in sugar, a scarce and expensive commodity from which he hoped to reap a handsome profit.

In 1863, fearing for the safety of his family (which by then included a son and two daughters of his own; a fourth daughter would be born in 1865), McLean moved to Appomattox Court House, where he would have ready access to both rail and communication lines to conduct his business and where he believed, wrongly it turned out, that no army was ever likely to appear. In the fall of 1865 Timothy O'Sullivan photographed Wilmer, his wife, her two older daughters, young Lula McLean, and Lula's sister Nannie on the front porch and steps of their home *(below)*.

Lt. Col. Ely S. Parker, who drafted the official copies of the terms Lee and Grant signed that led to the surrender of the Army of Northern Virginia and, for all practical purposes, ended the Civil War, was a 37-year-old Seneca Indian chief from the Tonawanda Reservation in western New York. Although trained in the law, he was not allowed to practice because Indians were not considered citizens. He and Grant had been close friends since before the war, when Grant was a store clerk in Galena, Illinois. With Grant's help, Parker became a captain of engineers in the U.S. Army. In August 1864 he joined Grant's staff as personal military secretary with the rank of lieutenant colonel, which a reporter called "a partial reward for invaluable services." Parker is shown here in late 1867, after he was promoted to brigadier general and served as a government emissary to various western Indian tribes.

Lt. Col. Charles Marshall, who accompanied Lee to the McLean house and drafted Lee's letter accepting Grant's surrender terms, was born October 2, 1830, in Warrenton, Virginia. He was the great-nephew of John Marshall, chief justice of the United States, 1801-35. After graduating from the University of Virginia in 1849, Marshall taught for a while at Indiana University before beginning to study law. In 1854 he joined a Baltimore, Maryland, law firm, from which he resigned after the war began. He joined Lee's staff as an aide-de-camp in March 1862 when Lee was military adviser to President Jefferson Davis, and his legal training proved useful in drafting military legislation to be submitted to the Confederate Congress. After Lee assumed command of the Army of Northern Virginia, Marshall's duties involved the collecting and collating of material for Lee's dispatches and preparing drafts of those dispatches. It was Marshall who wrote out Lee's April 9 letter to Grant requesting a suspension of hostilities to discuss surrendering the Army of Northern Virginia.

Lee was dressed in a new uniform and wore a handsome sword," he began. "His tall, commanding form thus set off contrasted strongly with the short figure of General Grant, clothed as he was in a soiled suit, without sword or other insignia of his position except a pair of dingy shoulder-straps." Lee's countenance betrayed no emotion. "As he was a man of much dignity, with an impassible face" wrote Grant, "it was impossible to say whether he felt inwardly glad that the end had finally come, or felt sad over the result, and was too manly to show it." After a few minutes of small talk, Lee reminded Grant why they were meeting and asked him to "commit to writing the terms you have proposed, so that they may be formally acted upon."

Grant asked an aide for writing materials and rapidly put terms to paper that reflected Lincoln's thinking about extending mercy to a beaten foe. The key provisions, as slightly amended at Lee's suggestion, stipulated that officers would "give their individual paroles not to take up arms against the Government of the United States until properly exchanged and each company or regimental commander sign a like parole for the men of their commands. The Arms, Artillery and public property to be parked and stacked and turned over to the officer appointed by me to receive them. This will not embrace the side Arms of the officers nor their private horses or baggage. This done each officer and man will be allowed to return to their homes not to be disturbed by United States Authority so long as they observe their parole and the laws in force where they may reside." Lee appreciated Grant's generosity about officers' arms and animals but pointed out that many Confederate cavalrymen and artillerists also owned their horses and would need them for the spring planting. Grant promised a separate order "to let every man of the Confederate army who claimed to own a horse or mule take the animal to his home."

While Grant's staff prepared two drafts of the final document, Lee instructed Marshall to compose a letter of acceptance. The generals passed a few more minutes discussing some Federal prisoners in Confederate hands and the pervasive hunger among Lee's soldiers. Grant offered to supply 25,000 rations for the famished troops. He then signed both copies of the surrender terms. Lee signed the letter Marshall

Sometime before Lee and Grant met in the McLean parlor to discuss surrender terms, seven-year-old Lula McLean left her favorite doll (below) on the sofa. It remained in the room throughout the negotiations. When the meeting ended, Union officers, anxious to obtain souvenirs of the event, appropriated various items from the room, including Lula's rag doll, which was taken by Lt. Col. Thomas W. C. Moore of Sheridan's staff.

Lula's sister Nannie later recounted that the officers who carried off McLean possessions had paid very little for them. The doll was donated to Appomattox Court House National Historical Park in 1992 and is now a permanent exhibit entitled "The Silent Witness."

Lee departed the McLean house as unceremoniously as he had come. After mounting Traveller and giving Grant and his officers a parting salute, the Confederate commander rode slowly from the McLean yard accompanied by his military secretary Charles Marshall and Marshall's courier, Pvt. Joshua O. Jones of the 39th Battalion Virginia Cavalry, Lee's headquarters guard. As Lee returned to the Confederate camp, "whole lines of men rushed down to the roadside and crowded around him to shake his hand. All tried to show the veneration and esteem in which they held him." Later, Lee and his staff signed a parole *(far left)* agreeing not to bear arms against the United States. Details of the formal surrender, scheduled for April 12, were drafted *(near left)* by special commissioners, three officers from each side, delegated to work out the details of the ceremony: Gens. William N. Pendleton, John B. Gordon, and James Longstreet for the Confederates, and Gens. John Gibbon, Charles Griffin, and Wesley Merritt for the Federals. The pencil stub was used by General Lee during the surrender meeting with General Grant.

KEITH ROCCO '01

> *"Everybody understood that the war was over... [and] officers and men shook hands and congratulated each other."*

Axel Leatz, captain, 5th New York Veteran Infantry, Army of the Potomac, U.S.A., April 9, 1865

had prepared. With the exchange of these documents, the Army of Northern Virginia, for nearly three years the greatest symbol of Confederate military power, ceased to exist.

Lee rose to leave shortly after 3 p.m. He and Grant shook hands. Stepping onto the porch, he returned the salute of Federal soldiers in McLean's yard. Horace Porter of Grant's staff stated that Lee paused, stared in the direction of his army's position across the Appomattox River, and "thrice smote the palm of his left hand slowly with his right fist in an absent sort of way." (Another witness, however, who stood within a few feet of the Confederate commander, had the impression that Lee's gloves were too small and "the 'smoting' referred to was such as anyone usually would do with a pair of tight fitting gloves.") Calling for an orderly to bring Traveller, Lee gently brushed the animal's forelock and mounted. Grant and the other Federal officers removed their hats as a gesture of respect. Lee lifted his hat in return before riding slowly away. Not long after Lee's departure, Grant telegraphed Secretary of War Stanton: "General Lee surrendered the Army of Northern Virginia this afternoon on terms proposed by myself."

Soldiers in both armies reacted swiftly to news of the surrender. Some Federals began a 100-gun salute, which Grant stopped because the "Confederates were now our prisoners, and we did not want to exult over their downfall." But thousands of his men, nearly as drained as their foe after the preceding week's brutal pace, openly expressed a mixture of delight and relief that the slaughter had ended. One soldier, whose diary on April 8 spoke of his being "completely tierd [sic] out and feet badly blistered," recorded that "Every one seemed to give himself up to all sorts of gymnastic manifestations of joy." A Union officer described how General Meade, who had been ill and traveling in an ambulance before learning of the surrender about 4 p.m., "rode like mad down the road with hat off shouting: 'The war is over, and we are going home!'" "I cried and laughed by turns," this man added. "I was never so happy in my life." Some took a more restrained view. Artillery Col. Charles S. Wainwright, though thankful for the result, wished the campaign had ended differently. "Could the war have been closed with such a battle as Gettysburg," he wrote, "it would have been more glorious for us; more in accordance with what poetical justice would seem to owe to the Army of the Potomac. As it is, the rebellion has been worn out rather than suppressed."

Confederate reactions fell across a broad spectrum. When Lee returned to his lines many soldiers crowded around Traveller, voicing continued devotion to their general and to the Confederacy. Others shouted their anger, including the man famously quoted by Maj. Gen. Bryan Grimes of Gordon's corps: "Blow, Gabriel, blow! My God, let him blow, I am ready to die!" The most common response among Lee's benumbed troops probably was relief that a hellish week of flight and privation had ended.

Intermittent rain returned on April 10, a day that wove arresting minor threads into the broader tapestry of Appomattox. Federals set up presses in Clover Hill Tavern that eventually printed 30,000 parole forms. Grant sought a last interview with Lee, and the two met about 10 a.m. Writing almost immediately after the fact, an eyewitness noted that "the meeting took place near a small stream, in the road"— almost certainly on a ridge just east of the village overlooking the headwaters of the Appomattox River. They remained mounted for the discussion, during which Grant asked Lee's help in securing the surrender of other Confederate military forces. Only President Davis could decide such questions, replied Lee, echoing Grant's comments on April 8 about the relative authority he and President Lincoln held. The men parted after about 30 minutes. Shortly before noon, Grant and his staff left Appomattox for Burkeville, whence they could board an eastbound train for Petersburg.

Lee issued a heartfelt farewell to his soldiers later in the day. Drafted by Colonel Marshall and revised by Lee, General Order No. 9 attributed Confederate defeat to the enemy's "overwhelming numbers and resources" and closed with an expression of "unceasing admiration" for the men's "constancy and devotion to your Country, and a grateful remembrance of your kind and generous consideration for myself...." Lee remained in camp near Appomattox until departing for Richmond on the morning of April 12 (some sources indicate that he left the previous morning) and played no further role regarding the formal surrender.

On the ride back to his headquarters from the McLean house, Grant realized that in the rush to finalize details of Lee's surrender he had forgotten to notify the War Department of the day's events. Dismounting, he sat down by the roadside and wrote this telegram to Secretary of War Edwin M. Stanton. It read: "Gen. Lee surrendered the Army of Northern Va. this afternoon on terms proposed by myself. The accompanying additional correspondence will show the conditions fully."

John R. Chapin made this sketch *(above)* of the April 12 surrender ceremony. The Confederate infantry, led by Maj. Gen. John B. Gordon *(top, left)*, stack their arms in front of Union troops of the First Division, Fifth Corps, Army of the Potomac. The Federal commander for the occasion was Brig. Gen. Joshua L. Chamberlain *(top, right)*, a former college professor from Maine turned soldier. Chamberlain, who appears in the sketch mounted in front of the Federal line, afterwards wrote his sister: "We received them with honor due to troops, at the shoulder and in silence. They came to a shoulder on passing my flag & preserved perfect order." The returning of the salute Chamberlain later called "honor answering honor."

Three generals from each army met in McLean's house on the 10th to draw up a blueprint for the ceremonial laying-down-of-arms two days later. Their work applied only to the Confederate infantry. More than 1,500 cavalrymen and 2,600 artillerists relinquished their weapons on April 10 and 11 respectively. The animals that pulled Confederate guns, limbers, and caissons had suffered more cruelly than the men. By April 12, wrote Porter Alexander, "many were down & many were dead from starvation. It was a pitiable sight." The bulk of Grant's forces would not be present for the ceremony on April 12. Sheridan and most of the cavalry marched toward Prospect Station on the afternoon of April 10, and the Second and Sixth Corps departed for Petersburg the next day. The First Division of the Fifth Corps would represent the United States at the surrender, with Brig. Gen. Joshua L. Chamberlain overseeing the details of the ceremony.

The 14 regiments of the division moved into position before dawn on April 12. As first sunlight broke above the horizon just past 5:30, their well-dressed ranks stretched for more than a quarter-mile along both sides of the Richmond-Lynchburg Stage Road. The right end of the line, occupied by Chamberlain's brigade, extended northward past the Peers house with the 32nd Massachusetts Infantry nearest the Confederates. The other flank rested west of the courthouse near Wilmer McLean's yard. Recent rains had left the road muddy. A damp chill lingered as muted light penetrated overhanging clouds.

Across the Appomattox River, Lee's veterans bestirred themselves, shuffling into their regimental formations for one last time. Eyewitnesses disagreed about the precise order of the Confederate march, but John Gordon's Second Corps certainly took the lead, filing onto the stage road and marching down the northern bank of the Appomattox River. The men splashed across the modest stream and ascended toward the village. Chamberlain and his staff, posted near the right flank of the 32nd Massachusetts, watched the progress of Gordon's column. In a letter written the next day, the former college professor, whose 20th Maine Infantry had earned renown on the slopes of Little Round Top, described the solemn scene. His soldiers offered "the honors due to troops," their weapons "at the shoulder & in si-

"If the one army drank the joy of victory and the other the bitter draught of defeat, it was a joy moderated by the recollection of the cost at which it had been purchased."

William Swinton, reporter, New York *Times*, recalling the events of April 9, 1865

lence." The Confederates "came to a shoulder on passing my flag & preserved perfect order." A member of the 32nd Massachusetts recorded a drill that would be repeated by each southern unit that made the dolorous trek: "[T]he gallant but defeated foe advanced in front the length of our line, then faced us, stacked arms, laid colors and equipments on stack, then marched away to make room for another line...." A soldier in the 155th Pennsylvania Infantry, posted west of the courthouse, estimated that about six hours passed before the last Confederates had laid down their weapons. "Not an unkind word was spoken to them," he said, "some of their color bearers shed tears when they delivered up their colors."

Although a precise count will never be known, approximately 21,000 to 22,000 Confederates participated in the ceremony on April 12. The number of paroled Confederates of all arms totaled 28,231, most of whom had their documents in hand by April 15. Those stark numbers highlight both the fragility of the army that left Richmond and Petersburg on April 2 and the impact of Grant's unrelenting pressure. Lee had seen fully half of his fabled army disappear in the course of a single week.

Events at Appomattox immediately took on immense symbolic importance. In a narrow sense, Lee had done no more than surrender a fraction of the Confederacy's soldiers. Johnston's army remained intact in North Carolina, as did many smaller forces scattered across the southern landscape. Yet Lee and the Army of Northern Virginia loomed so large—as the Confederacy's primary national institution and the Union's principal enemy—that most people, North and South, believed its surrender marked the end of the war. A pair of civilian witnesses captured the tenor of countless reactions. From New York City on April 9, diarist George Templeton Strong's first response was "LEE AND HIS ARMY HAVE SURRENDERED! Gloria in Excelcis Deo." Two days later, Strong recorded that "[p]eople hold the war virtually ended. It looks so. Lee is out of the game. Napoleon could hardly save Joe Johnston's army." Georgian Eliza Frances Andrews painted a dreary picture as rumors of Lee's surrender swirled through the southern home front: "No one seems to doubt it, and everybody feels ready to give up hope. 'It is useless to struggle longer,' seems to be the common cry, and the poor wounded men go hobbling about the streets with despair on their faces."

Grant and Lee set important precedents at Appomattox. Although he deplored the Confederate cause "as one of the worst for which a people ever fought," Grant honored Lincoln's hopes for a compassionate peace by offering generous paroles to Lee and his army. A few weeks later, in the wake of Lincoln's assassination, President Andrew Johnson threatened retributive hangings of Lee and other Confederate generals. Grant responded with a threat of his own. He would resign if the President violated Lee's protection under the agreement at Appomattox. For his part, Lee's insistence on a surrender that acknowledged Union military triumph sent a clear message across the Confederacy that resorting to guerrilla warfare was not an option. Deep wells of bitterness remained among soldiers and citizens on both sides. It could not have been otherwise at the close of a four-year war of overwhelming magnitude. Grant and Lee might have stoked that bitterness with a different handling of the surrender. They chose instead to craft an agreement with the best interests of their peoples firmly in mind.

"I felt like anything rather than rejoicing at the downfall of a foe who had fought so long and so valiantly."

Ulysses S. Grant on accepting the surrender of the Army of Northern Virginia, April 9, 1865

Harper's Weekly *artist Alfred Waud sketched General Lee and Colonel Marshall as they rode away from the McLean House, April 9, 1865.*

Part 3

An America Transformed

By David W. Blight

On May 18, 1865, a week after President Andrew Johnson proclaimed "armed resistance to the authority of this Government" to be "virtually at an end," orders were issued by the adjutant-general for a grand review by the President and other government officials of Maj. Gen. George G. Meade's Army of the Potomac and Maj. Gen. William T. Sherman's Army of Georgia. For most of two days, May 23 and 24, company after company, regiment after regiment, marched in orderly fashion from the Capitol to the White House, where a reviewing stand had been set up along Pennsylvania Avenue.

Preceding pages: *On the 50th anniversary of "Pickett's Charge" at Gettysburg, Union and Confederate survivors of that encounter shake hands across the stone wall on Cemetery Ridge. Reunions like these helped heal many of the emotional wounds between the two sections.*

The final April of the Civil War left Americans on both sides with conflicting emotions: exhilaration mixed with dread, relief with lingering hatreds, and confusion about the future with a host of untried ideas about putting the country back together again. Just at the dawn of peace, only 48 hours after Lee's surviving troops stacked their muskets at Appomattox, President Abraham Lincoln was assassinated in Washington by a Confederate partisan, ushering in a long period of national mourning and bitterness Americans had never experienced. In an emerging, lethal mixture of raw war memories and hatreds bred of four years of desperate strife, the surrender at Appomattox settled into American history as a signal event that most people would never forget. Time might pass by the little village of Appomattox Court House but not the remembrance of its few days of somber glory.

For many white Southerners, stunned by a sense of total personal and material loss, the end of the war and the death of Lincoln brought psychological trauma, fear for their futures, souls torn between feelings of vindictiveness and the hope of relief and recovery. White Southerners faced utter defeat as perhaps no other Americans ever have. Many had fled their plantations and farms before the Union armies in Virginia, Georgia, or the Lower Mississippi River valley. In Tyler, Texas, on April 28, while living in exile from her Louisiana plantation, Kate Stone wrote in her journal of General Lee's rumored surrender. "All are fearfully depressed," she reported. "I cannot bear to hear them talk of defeat." She still hoped that Confederate armies might rally and fight "to be free or die." On May 15 Stone opened a journal entry with a definition of the South's immediate fate that no doubt spoke for many, especially women living in isolation and physical hardship: "Conquered, Submission, Subjugation are the words that burn into my heart, and yet I feel that we are

Many southerners were unable to accept the defeat of the Confederacy. One of these was Edmund Ruffin, agricultural reformer and outspoken southern nationalist, who considered slavery the cornerstone of southern society. As early as 1850 he had begun to champion secession as the South's only hope of salvation.

As an honorary member of South Carolina's Palmetto Guards, Ruffin was accorded the opportunity of firing one of the first shots against Fort Sumter on April 12, 1861. On June 17, 1865, reduced to virtual destitution by the war and despondent over Lee's surrender and his own declining health, he committed suicide rather than live in a reunited Union with "the perfidious, malignant and vile Yankee race."

doomed to know them in all their bitterness." Stone rejoiced in Lincoln's death and honored John Wilkes Booth for ridding "the world of a tyrant.... We are glad he is not alive to rejoice in our humiliation and insult us with his jokes."

In the chaos and despair after Lee's surrender, Confederate soldiers, many malnourished and ill, trudged toward their homes. Confederate Gen. James Longstreet watched the remnants of his men stack their arms and fold their flags at Appomattox, as they then "walked empty-handed to find their distant, blighted homes." And after his release from prison in Boston in October 1865, former Confederate Vice-President Alexander H. Stephens rode a slow train southward toward his home in Georgia. He described a landscape in ruin everywhere. In northern Virginia the "desolation of the country... was horrible to behold." And in northern Georgia Stephens declared the "desolation...heart-sickening. Fences gone, fields all a-waste, houses burnt." In many regions of the South ex-Confederates faced the problem of material and spiritual hopelessness, the desperate need to revive agriculture and civil society as quickly as possible.

Many Confederate officers and their families, fearing arrest and trial for treason, or for refusing to participate in the new social order, fled the country during the months following the war. An estimated 8,000 to 10,000 chose exile, some temporarily and many permanently, in Mexico, Brazil, England, Canada, in parts of Central and South America, and even as far as Japan. Confederate ruin was more than some white Southerners could bear. Joel Chandler Harris, who would later become a famous dialect writer of folktales and create the character Uncle Remus, was a teenage boy in a small Georgia village at war's end. Southern defeat came like thunder claps, Harris later wrote. "The last trump will cause no greater surprise and consternation...than the news of Lee's surrender caused.... The public mind had not been prepared...the curtain came down and the lights went out...." Many Southerners had seen defeat coming for months, and the degree of desertion in early 1865 in Confederate armies attests to this growing realization. But what would follow in the post-war South was a matter of dread to most former Confederates, especially in the wake of the revolution of black emancipation. Kate Stone considered the prospect of "Negro equality" an "unendurable fate." And in lowcountry Georgia, a young planter woman, Eva Jones, described her family in shock that "slavery is entirely abolished," and the realization a source of "all enveloping sorrow." Her sister-in-law, Caroline Jones, also felt "almost paralyzed" by events and took solace from the "righteous retribution upon Lincoln."

But black and white Northerners, and other supporters of the Union cause, had very different reactions to the end of the war and the tragedy of Lincoln's murder. The week after the surrender and the assassination, in Vicksburg, Mississippi, as in a thousand other places, a large crowd of ex-slaves, in silence and tears, gathered in front of a store window that contained a photograph of Lincoln. A black correspondent from Chicago tried to characterize the scene of Lincoln's funeral procession in that deeply Southern city. "The grandeur was beyond description," he remarked. "The colored citizens turned out in full force, and were well-received.... We can only look on in breathless silence, and think of the great change." Blacks across the land felt great exhilaration and anxiety at such change. A month after Appomattox, a black Union soldier, Corp. William Gibson of the 28th U.S. Colored Troops, wrote from City Point, Virginia, worrying that his home state of Indiana might not remove its old "Black Laws" from its statute books. Aware that racism knew no geographical boundaries in America, Gibson nevertheless seemed flushed with hope over the "rights" he believed his "old 28th" had earned. "We ask to be made equal before the law," said the veteran, "grant us this, and we ask no more. Let the friends of freedom canvas the country on this subject. Let the sound go into all the earth."

In Boston, a white diarist, Caroline Barrett White, followed the final dramas of the war with keen interest. On April 10, 1865, she recorded: "Hurrah! Hurrah! 'Sound the loud timbal o'er Egypt's dark sea'— early this morning our ears were greeted with the sound of bells ringing a joyous peal—Gen. Lee had surrendered with his whole army to Gen. Grant! Surely this is the Lord's doing and it is 'marvelous in our eyes.'" In biblical cadences and with effusive patriotism, White described "general jubilation"

"Everything is in a state of disorganization and tumult. We have no currency, no law save the primitive code that might makes right.... The suspense and anxiety in which we live are terrible."

Eliza Andrews, Georgia resident, May 2, 1865

around the New England city. But then on Saturday, April 15, she recorded different news: "The darkest day I ever remember. This morning the sun rose upon a nation jubilant with victory, but it sets upon one plunged into deepest sorrow." In her longest of all diary entries during the war period, White described the "shocking intelligence" of Lincoln's murder. "Where will treason end," she asked in despair. "The rapidity with which events crowd upon one another is perfectly bewildering." During the period of Lincoln's funerals, White continued to express her anger and sorrow—over all the death and sacrifice in the war. "I have felt very sad all day but have kept any feelings pent up as well as possible," she wrote on April 19. Just what to do with all these feelings of sorrow and loathing was a challenge Americans faced all across the war-torn country in those weeks and months after Appomattox. With time, many would fashion lasting images of the surrender at Appomattox as the beginning of peace and reconciliation between the sections. But we should not mistake the long-term need of national reunion for the short-term agonies and hatreds that festered in post-war America.

From the broadest perspective, the Civil War wrought from all its suffering a transformation of American society and government. In real and disputed ways, what so many Americans, North and South, had long referred to as the old "Union" now had the potential to become a modern "nation." The states' rights tradition, the struggle to find the right balance in any historical context between federal and state power, has never ceased in our constitutional history. Indeed, before the war Northerners and Southerners had both appealed to states' rights doctrine, and it would experience a fierce revival in 20th-century struggles over racial segregation. But the idea of secession was buried seemingly forever in the surrender field at Appomattox.

Because of the imperatives of war, the United States became a more centralized government, affecting the daily lives of Americans as never before. Through tax, banking, and tariff legislation during the war, the American economy emerged after 1865 as more nationalized. The expanded role of the federal government to fight a total war brought similar expansion in its control over graduated income taxes, a centralized monetary system, agricultural policy, the creation of land-grant colleges, homesteading on federal lands, immigration laws, and the building of the transcontinental railroad.

Similarly, as Americans tried to imagine their future in the wake of their most divisive experience, they were living in an age of new technologies, an era when machines would come increasingly to control, with great anxiety, communication, transportation, and industrial production. Much would seem newly standardized to rural farmers and city workers, like railroad schedules and the federal soldiers' pension system. But the centralization of government did not abate the growth of "big business" and the pursuit of wealth, which fell more and more into the hands of a few. Indeed, the industrial age to which the war helped give birth would be defined by new strife between labor and capital and over how to define the limits of racial equality. From the end of the war until the turn of the 20th century and beyond, Americans would face the recurring boom and bust cycle of an unregulated, modernizing economy reaching abroad to become a world power. Appomattox, indeed, was a historical marker of much more than the triumph and defeat of armies and the beginning of Reconstruction.

The Reconstruction period (1865-1877) was one long referendum on the meaning and memory of the verdict reached at Appomattox. The Union armies had won the war decisively on the battlefield. But what would be the meaning of this war that had destroyed slavery and forced the nation to consider a redefinition of the very nature of the American republic? Would the nation undergo a "rebirth," as Lincoln had called for in his "Gettysburg Address," around the principle of racial equality? Or, would it rapidly restore the Southern states to the Union with little Constitutional and social change? Differing visions of America's future were at stake. In 1862 the New England philosopher, Ralph Waldo Emerson, had called the war "a new glass to see all old things through...our sole and doleful instructor." In the wake of the surrender in April 1865, however, Emerson was anxious about just what Reconstruction would bring. "Tis far best that the rebels have been pounded instead of negotiated into a peace," he wrote. "They must remember it.... I fear that the

> *"Neither slavery nor involuntary servitude, except as a punishment for crime..., shall exist within the United States, or any place subject to their jurisdiction."*
>
> 13th Amendment, U.S. Constitution, December 18, 1865

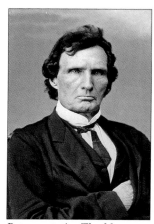

Representative Thaddeus Stevens of Pennsylvania rejected President Andrew Johnson's lenient Reconstruction policies, fought to secure full civil rights for the recently freed slaves, and helped draft the 14th Amendment.

Senator Charles Sumner of Massachusetts also opposed Johnson's policies and argued in Congress for legislation to allow Southern plantations to be taken from their owners and divided among former slaves.

high tragic historic justice which the nation...should execute, will be softened...and toasted away at dinner tables. But the problems that now remain to be solved are very intricate and perplexing." Those perplexing post-war problems made the Reconstruction era one Americans have often wished to forget rather than confront.

The great challenge of Reconstruction was to determine how a national blood feud of horrible human cost could be reconciled at the same time a new nation emerged out of war and social revolution. The survivors on both sides, winners and losers in the fullest sense, would still inhabit the same land and eventually live under the same government. The task was harrowing: how to square black freedom and the stirrings of racial equality in law with a cause (the South's) that had lost almost everything except its unbroken belief in white supremacy. During Reconstruction, Americans faced a nearly overwhelming task: how to understand the tangled relationship between two essential ideas—healing and justice.

Healing, both sectional and personal, and justice, both for the freed people and for those who had been victims of total war (white Southerners more than anyone), had to occur. But these two aims of healing and justice never developed in historical balance in post-war America. As Sen. Henry Wilson of Massachusetts expressed it in 1867, Reconstruction was a "conflict of ideas" as well as of "passions, prejudices, and bitter memories," all of which had to be faced and somehow reconciled between former enemies sharing the same political future. As that future was being debated fiercely in Congress and across the country, Edward A. Pollard, wartime editor of the Richmond *Examiner*, wrote his long manifesto, *The Lost Cause*, published in 1867. Pollard issued a warning to all who would ever attempt to shape policy or structure the memory of the war. "All that is left the South," wrote Pollard, "is the war of ideas." The war may have decided the "restoration of the union and the excision of slavery," he declared, "but the war did not decide Negro equality." With such obstacles in their path, Americans tried to determine what the results of the war truly were.

The story of Reconstruction took place on two different fronts. One was the political and Constitutional crisis over who would shape policy and just what that policy would be in Washington, D.C. The other front was within the South itself, on the ground, where former slaveowners and former slaves had to establish new social, economic, and political relations. On both of these fronts Americans entered uncharted waters. Well before the war had ended, President Lincoln had proposed a plan of Reconstruction that would be rapid and relatively lenient to former Confederates, and which would involve at least some place for black voting rights. Lincoln greatly feared recurrent guerrilla warfare and he hoped to keep Reconstruction policy under Presidential authority. Hence, his attempts to create new Southern states with as few as 10 percent of their "loyal" citizens taking oaths to the Union, drafting new constitutions, and then readmitting them to the Union. But before he died, Lincoln was already opposed by the "Radicals" in his own Republican party, led in the Senate by Charles Sumner of Massachusetts, and in the House of Representatives by Thaddeus Stevens of Pennsylvania. Sumner and Stevens fashioned a very different vision of Reconstruction, one that would put the former Confederate states under federal occupation, require majorities to take loyalty oaths, and require broader change in black civil and political rights. Some Radical Republicans also hoped for significant land confiscation and redistribution to the freed people.

The Radicals saw Reconstruction as the opportunity to convert black freedom into genuine citizenship, economic self-reliance, and political liberty. They viewed the former Confederate states as "conquered provinces," which had to be re-invented as states and readmitted to the Union by Congress. They intended to broaden education in the South, among blacks and whites, and to forge a more democratic civic culture. The Republicans hoped they would have an ally in Lincoln's successor, Andrew Johnson, but they quickly learned they did not. Although elected as a Southern Democrat to the U.S. Senate in 1857 from Tennessee, Johnson was the only senator from a seceded state who refused to follow his state out of the Union in 1861. It was Johnson's Unionism that prompted Lincoln to put him on the ticket as his running mate in 1864. Although he had opposed secession as a drastic mis-

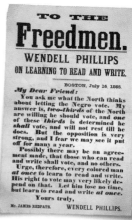

Boston reformer Wendell Phillips's July 16, 1865, letter to radical abolitionist James Redpath on the urgency of preparing former slaves and other blacks to vote was made into this broadside for widest possible distribution and influence. During the war Phillips had criticized President Lincoln for his moderate stand on emancipation, arguing that the government owed blacks not only their freedom but land, education, and full civil rights as well.

Andrew Johnson, a southerner and a racist, urged a mild Reconstruction policy that would not punish the South but help it recover quickly from the devastating effects of the war. His attempts to block efforts to force southern states to guarantee full equality for blacks set the stage for a showdown with radical congressional Republicans who considered black voting rights as crucial to establishing their power base in the South. At Johnson's impeachment trial in 1868, Charles Sumner called him "the impersonation of the tyrannical slave power."

take for the South (which many did in his native eastern Tennessee), Johnson was an ardent states' rightist. He favored limited government, and above all, when it came to race, Johnson was a thoroughgoing white supremacist. He shared none of the Radicals' expansive conception of federal power; he stated his philosophy toward Reconstruction in the slogan: "The Constitution as it is, and the Union as it was."

Johnson controlled Reconstruction during 1865 and attempted to restore the ex-Confederate states to the Union with very little of Southern society reshaped. The "Johnson governments," ready in his view for readmission by December 1865, included the notorious "Black Codes," laws written across the South restricting the freedmen's economic options and mobility, and utterly denying them any political liberty. Evidence suggests that in the first year after the war, in the chaos of defeat and destitution, if compelled, many white Southerners may have been willing to accept harsh terms and revolutionary changes as requirements for re-entry into the United States. But with Johnson's encouragements to defiance, most ex-Confederates insisted that they should control their own conditions of restitution to national membership. Outraged at the sheer leniency of Johnson's approach to Reconstruction, the Republican leadership of Congress refused to readmit the Southern states in December 1865. For the next two years, they locked horns with the President in an unprecedented Constitutional struggle over federal policy, the outcome of which would, indeed, reconstruct the Union initially on the Radicals' terms, but also ultimately foment a successful white counterrevolution across the South throughout the 1870s.

The Radical Republicans' blueprint for Reconstruction was based on a political philosophy grounded in the idea of an activist federal government, a guarantee of black male suffrage, and a faith in free labor. The Radicals envisioned Reconstruction as a process of remaking a nation by remaking the defeated South. Their cardinal principle was equality before the law, which in 1866 they enshrined in the 14th Amendment, expanding citizenship to all those born in the United States without regard to race. That same year Congress also renewed the Bureau of

Refugees, Freedmen, and Abandoned Lands (the Freedmen's Bureau), and passed the first civil rights act in American history. Congress had created the Freedmen's Bureau, an unprecedented agency of social uplift necessitated by the ravages of the war, just a month before Lee's surrender. Americans had never engaged in federal aid to citizens on such a scale.

With thousands of refugees, white and black, displaced in the South, the government continued what private freedmen's aid societies had started as early as 1862. During its four-year existence, the Freedmen's Bureau supplied food and medical services, built several thousand schools and some colleges, negotiated several hundred thousand employment contracts between freedmen and their former masters, and tried to manage confiscated land. The Bureau was a controversial aspect of Reconstruction, within the South, where whites generally hated it, and within the Federal Government where politicians were divided over its constitutionality (Johnson opposed it strongly on grounds that it violated states' rights). Some Bureau agents were devoted to freedmen's rights, and others were opportunists who exploited the chaos of Southern agriculture and race and labor relations. Americans were relatively inexperienced at the Freedmen's Bureau's task—social reform through military occupation.

In Appomattox County itself, Freedmen's Bureau agents, as well as Union officers, confronted problems of social disorder in the immediate wake of the surrender. A horseman passing through the county on April 29, 1865, described "one eternal scene of desolation & destruction" along a 13-mile route. The armies had left hundreds of dead horses and mules and burned every fence rail for miles. A Freedmen's Bureau post was established in Lynchburg to try to settle disputes over remaining livestock, to stop plundering and marauding in the countryside, and especially to try to establish new labor arrangements for the freedmen. Many blacks were eager to test the limits of their new freedom; they were reluctant to sign annual labor contracts or to work for uncertain wages. They had come to believe that the Federal army would redistribute land to them as their own property. While most whites clung to the belief that former slaves would not

"We want peace and good order at the South; but it can only come by the fullest recognition of the rights of all classes."

Blanche K. Bruce, ex-slave and U.S. Senator from Mississippi, March 31, 1876

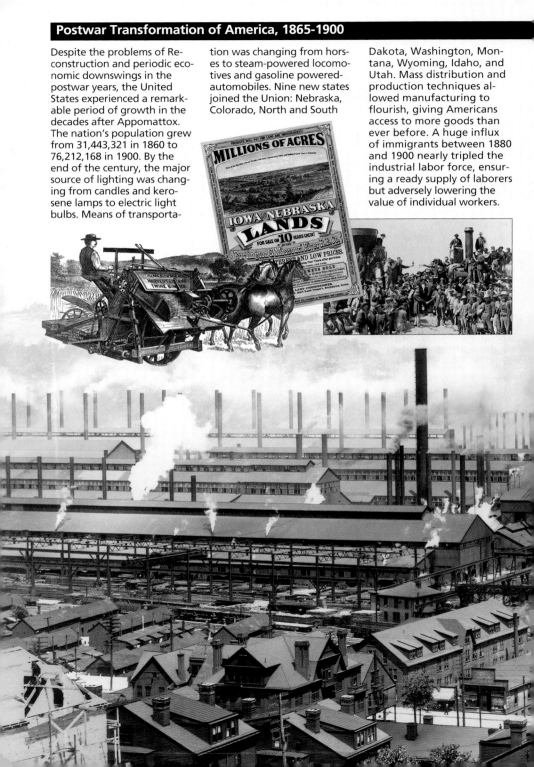

Postwar Transformation of America, 1865-1900

Despite the problems of Reconstruction and periodic economic downswings in the postwar years, the United States experienced a remarkable period of growth in the decades after Appomattox. The nation's population grew from 31,443,321 in 1860 to 76,212,168 in 1900. By the end of the century, the major source of lighting was changing from candles and kerosene lamps to electric light bulbs. Means of transportation was changing from horses to steam-powered locomotives and gasoline powered-automobiles. Nine new states joined the Union: Nebraska, Colorado, North and South Dakota, Washington, Montana, Wyoming, Idaho, and Utah. Mass distribution and production techniques allowed manufacturing to flourish, giving Americans access to more goods than ever before. A huge influx of immigrants between 1880 and 1900 nearly tripled the industrial labor force, ensuring a ready supply of laborers but adversely lowering the value of individual workers.

Thanks to new methods of processing iron into steel, the steel industry flourished in western Pennsylvania and eastern Ohio. Until new sources of ore were discovered in Michigan, Minnesota, Alabama, and elsewhere, Pittsburgh was the country's steelmaking center and the sprawling Carnegie Steel Plant *(below)* in Homestead, Pennsylvania, the largest steel mill. The steel industry's need for lubrication for its machinery spurred expansion of the oil industry. Between 1859, when the first oil wells appeared *(right)*, and 1870, the annual production of oil soared from 2,000 barrels to nearly 10,000,000. Much of this early petroleum was used to produce kerosene for lighting.

The expansion of the railroads also stimulated the economy. The completion of the first transcontinental railroad in 1869 *(near left)* sparked a flurry of railroad construction. By 1890 four more transcontinental lines had been built and more than 200,000 miles of track linked America's cities, facilitating the movement of goods and people and carrying settlers westward to mine, farm, and ranch. Rail companies themselves, granted large tracts of land by federal and local governments, lured settlers into the West by selling excess lands cheap-

ly and offering cheap transportation and freight rates for shipping produce to market *(middle left)*. The development and refinement of labor-saving farm equipment, such as the reaper *(far left)*, invented by Cyrus McCormick in the 1830s and aggressively marketed in the postwar years, revolutionized agriculture by making frontier life easier for new settlers and allowing farmers to enjoy bigger harvests. All in all, the industrial and economic development of the postwar years increased the wealth and improved the lives of many, but not everyone—especially not freedmen, Southerners trying to recover from the war, or the American Indian, whose civilization would disappear in the wake of westward expansion.

The Ku Klux Klan, two of whose members are seen here "in disguise" from an 1868 issue of Harper's Weekly, *was organized by ex-Confederate elements to oppose the Reconstruction policies of Radical Republicans and to maintain, through intimidation and violence, white supremacy in the South after the Civil War. It was one of several vigilante organizations formed in many southern communities at a time when local government was weak or nonexistent and there were fears of black outrages. In many southern states, especially in the mountain and Piedmont areas, Klan violence succeeded in keeping black men from voting, allowing Democrats and ex-Confederates to gain political control.*

work unless compelled, most blacks wanted economic independence. John Dennett, a young Harvard-educated journalist, traveling and writing for the *Nation* magazine, spent considerable time in the counties around Appomattox and Lynchburg in August 1865. He interviewed many former slaveowners who complained bitterly of the "insubordination" of black laborers; some openly refused to pay wages at all and wished for a return to slavery. Dennett observed many freedmen requesting the Freedmen's Bureau to help them obtain land and mules. "Now, sir," said one freedman to a Bureau agent, "some of we would wish to hire land to work for ourself, or, perhaps, buy a piece of ground."

The great unanswered question of the Reconstruction years was how freedmen might acquire land. Most black farmers and laborers ultimately had to sacrifice their desire for independence in the system known as sharecropping. Since most of them lacked money to buy land, they preferred the next best thing: renting the land they worked. But the post-war South had a cash-poor economy with few sources of credit. Black farmers and white landowners therefore turned to a "share" system in which farmers kept part of their crop and gave the rest to the landowner while living on his property. The landlord or a merchant "furnished" food and supplies before the harvest and deducted the cost from the farmer's share when the landlord sold the crop.

The sharecropping system, which materialized widely by 1868-70, thus emerged as a compromise. Dennett observed such a contract arranged as early as 1865 in Appomattox County with "one half the crop to be his [the landowner's] and one half to be ours [the freedman's family]." The system eased landowners' problems with cash and credit, and provided them a permanent, dependent labor force; blacks accepted it because it seemed to release them from daily supervision. But sharecropping later proved to be a disaster. Owners and furnishing merchants developed a monopoly of control over the re-emergent agricultural economy, as sharecroppers found themselves mired in ever-increasing debt.

Meanwhile, the Union was politically restored. Wresting control of Reconstruction from President Johnson by 1867, Congress divided the 11 ex-Confederate states into five military districts and made black male suffrage a condition of readmission to the Union. By 1870 all ex-Confederate states had rejoined the Union, and in most, the Republican party, built as a coalition of "carpetbaggers" (Northerners who moved South), "scalawags" (native Southerners who gave allegiance to the new order), and black voters. The ballot, indeed, took on a profound significance to blacks as they became the core constituency of Southern Republicanism. With this newfound faith in politics blacks tried to fashion their post-slavery lives.

In February 1869 Congress passed the 15th Amendment, a limited guarantee of equal suffrage that forbade states from denying the right to vote on grounds of race or previous condition of servitude. But the amendment was silent on the 11 Northern states that still denied the vote to blacks; it also ignored women's suffrage, and most importantly, did nothing to stop future enactment of inequitable qualifications tests. Despite these limitations, many Northerners saw the 15th Amendment as a final act of Reconstruction.

Perhaps the most remarkable revolution during Radical Reconstruction was the degree of political mobilization in southern black communities and the emergence of a group of black politicians at nearly every level of government. Consisting of many freeborn, Northern-educated ministers, former soldiers, and activists (although some ex-slaves as well) more than 600 black men served in state legislatures and 16 in Congress during Reconstruction. These men helped to establish public school systems, more equitable taxation, and bargaining mechanisms between planters and laborers.

On the community level, especially in the pivotal election year of 1868, blacks attended rallies and meetings where Republican newspapers were read aloud, and speeches were delivered by dozens of black itinerant lecturers. At these exuberant meetings, blacks wrapped themselves in the heritage of the Declaration of Independence, as well as recollections of slavery, and claimed, as during an Alabama meeting, "exactly the same rights, privileges and immunities as are enjoyed by white men...the law no longer knows white or black, but simply men." Such were the freedmen's hopes for Reconstruction's transformations of America, but

By September 1867, in compliance with the Reconstruction Act of the previous March, officers of the Freedmen's Bureau had registered some 700,000 black men to vote. Their participation in the 1867 elections helped to elect delegates who would meet the following year to draw up new constitutions for the states of the former Confederacy. Alfred R. Waud captured some of these newly enfranchised citizens of the United States as they cast their first vote, "not with expressions of exultation or of defiance of their old masters and present opponents depicted on their countenances, but looking serious and solemn and determined."

Ulysses S. Grant entered the Presidency with little or no understanding of the powers and duties of the office. Once favoring a mild Reconstruction policy similar to Johnson's, by the time he became President Southern violence against freedmen and Unionists had led him to embrace the Radical Republicans, who had viewed the war as a fervent crusade against slavery and who were now advocating an expanded national authority in the South and immediate equal civil and political rights for blacks.

their days of power and security were short-lived.

In 1868 black votes were crucial to the election of Republican Ulysses S. Grant to the Presidency. Reconstruction policies depended directly upon the political will of Northerners to stay a course of federal enforcement of the new racial and legal order. "These constitutions and governments," declared a Charleston, South Carolina, opposition newspaper, "will last just as long as the bayonets which ushered them into being...." That year the Ku Klux Klan launched a campaign of political violence and terror directed at black and white Republicans. During Grant's first term (1869-73), a legal and military campaign against the Klan was temporarily effective, but only after such groups had committed hundreds of murders, tortures, and burnings of property in their effort to re-establish conservative white control of Southern politics.

During the 1870s the power of the Radical Republicans waned dramatically. Driven by an ideology of laissez-faire government and economic expansion (especially in the wake of the depression of 1873), and a desire to leave the South to its own devices, the Federal Government retreated from the egalitarian promises of Reconstruction. Aided by violence, used on a scale and as a tool of normal politics as in no other time of American history, a white counter-revolution, known as "Southern Redemption," occurred through the resurgent Democratic Party. The final retreat, and collapse of Reconstruction, came in the disputed election of 1876. Only three states—South Carolina, Florida, and Louisiana—remained under tenuous Republican control. Due to corruption and intimidation, the election returns in those states were fiercely disputed, leading to a late-hour national political compromise giving Republican Rutherford B. Hayes the Presidency in return for acquiescence in Democratic control ("home rule") of the remaining Southern states. This sectional deal, reached only a few days before Hayes's inauguration and under the threat of a new disunion, brought an irrevocable end to Reconstruction in the spring of 1877. Much of the country rejoiced that all the issues of the war and Reconstruction seemed now truly over. But these events had dire consequences for the legacies of emancipation and the Constitutional revolution the war had wrought. The ultimate tragedy of the era was that as the sections reconciled, the races divided. Strict segregation laws and direct disfranchisement of blacks were still a decade or two into the future. But Lee's retreat to and surrender at Appomattox had become in 12 years of turbulent Reconstruction a new and longer retreat by the whole of the American people from responsibility for the expansion of the freedom that Grant's forces had won in April 1865.

As the Civil War receded into the past in the late 19th century, a national reunion seemed to emerge in great part on Southern terms. A tradition developed known as the "Lost Cause," a romantic conception of what the Confederacy had fought for, a web of veterans' survivors' associations, women's memorial organizations, and ritual commemorations. It is often said that the Lost Cause was born at Appomattox in the compassionate character of the surrender terms, and in Lee's dignified departure from his army. The Lost Cause tradition was in its early years a psychological response to defeat among Southerners, a way of coping with their world turning upside down. But it also developed as an ideology, a set of arguments about the meaning of the war and who should control its legacies. In his farewell address, Lee had told his men that they had been "overwhelmed by superior numbers and resources." There is, of course, much truth in the claim that the North won because of manpower and its industrial might. But many former Confederates turned this idea into an explanation of why noble causes can lose, and of how the Confederacy was the true embodiment of the American Revolution in its stand for state sovereignty against centralized government.

Many Southerners also converted the Lost Cause ideology into an argument about the causes of the war, claiming that Confederates never really fought for slavery, and that theirs was a cause only of self-determination. Moreover, many diehard Lost Cause advocates converted this nostalgic yearning for another era into an argument for white supremacy in the present; they did so with story after story, admired by thousands of Northern readers, of an idyllic Old South of happy race relations on plantations where most blacks lived lives of faithful service to their benevolent masters. As early as 1868, E. A.

Rutherford B. Hayes assumed the Presidency after one of the most hostile and controversial political campaigns in American history. One month after taking office, he ordered Federal troops out of the South, ending Reconstruction in favor of "wise, honest, and peaceful local self-government." The return to home rule pleased Southern Democrats, who saw it as an opportunity for the South to regain its economic stability and weaken the growing political influence of black voters.

> *"The fundamental principle of this republic is that every citizen shall be equal before the law."*

George William Curtis, editor, *Harper's Weekly*, December 20, 1871

Pollard, in *The Lost Cause Regained*, counseled reconciliation with conservative Northerners on Southern terms. "To the extent of securing the supremacy of the white man," wrote Pollard, "and the traditional liberties of the country...she [the South] really triumphs in the true cause of the war." In these arguments, the Lost Cause ceased to be about "loss" at all, and became a victory narrative, a triumph over Reconstruction's experiment in racial equality in which all the nation could share. The Lost Cause became a tonic against fear of social change and it armed those determined to control, if not destroy, the rise of black people in the social order.

With time, the surrender at Appomattox itself became an important symbol of national reconciliation. It has been the peace begun there, and not the war ended, that Americans have most wanted to remember. The moving ceremony on the surrender field on April 12, 1865, the exchange of gestures of honor between Union Gen. Joshua L. Chamberlain and Confederate Gen. John B. Gordon, have long been a preferred memory to the enduring and unresolved legacies of the war. We have endlessly focussed on the ending of the fight, and all the soldiers' sacrifice, and not as easily on how American society coped with the long-term implications of total war and emancipation.

What happened at Appomattox between soldiers is a historical moment of authentic tragedy and grandeur. Its drama is irresistible. Indeed, swords were turned into saws and pen knives, so to speak, as soldiers and civilians carved away and uprooted the apple tree under which Grant and Lee had allegedly conducted their first meeting. When Grant himself came to write of the surrender in his famous *Memoirs* (1885), he, too, chose to remember the event in a reconciliationist tone. After his historic meeting with Lee at the McLean House, Grant ordered a cessation of any celebrations in his own army. He insisted on no "unnecessary humiliation" of the defeated Confederates. They "were now our prisoners, and we did not want to exult over their downfall." After 20 years, Grant could hardly contain his admiration for Lee, who seemed "too manly" to show his "feelings." But Grant remembered his own feelings in terms that may have reinforced both Lost Cause advocates and Yankee reconciliationists.

"My own feelings," wrote Grant, "which had been quite jubilant at the receipt of his [Lee's] letter, were sad and depressed. I felt like anything but rejoicing at the downfall of a foe who had fought so long and valiantly, and had suffered so much for a cause, though that cause was, I believe, one of the worst for which a people ever fought, and one for which there was the least excuse. I do not question, however, the sincerity of the great mass of those who were opposed to us." Here were the terms of the American reunion rendered in probably the most oft-read chapter of one of its best-selling works: shared grief at war's costs coupled with Northern respect for the sincerity of Southern devotion to their cause, even when that cause was judged repugnant. In Grant's suggestion of a kind of necessary forgetting, the war was nearly drained of political meaning. The reunion by the 1880s was a consummation forged out of soldiers' dignity—the blessed peace, surpassing politics, that Grant had driven Lee to help him create at Appomattox. Grant finished his *Memoirs* as he was dying of throat cancer at Mount McGregor in upstate New York, and his depiction of two mystic days at Appomattox mirrored the culture he was about to depart.

A generation later, in a popular novel, *Cease Firing* (1912), the Southern writer, Mary Johnston, a Virginian imbued with Lost Cause tradition and a determination to represent its complexities, imagined a telling dialogue that may have captured the memory that most Americans, then and perhaps since, desire to embrace about the Civil War. On the last page of the book, Lee's army is retreating west toward the surrender at Appomattox. The April breezes are not yet warm, and the rivers to be forded still run cold. One Confederate soldier asks another what he thinks it all [the war] means. "I think that we were both right and both wrong," says the veteran of many battles, "and that, in the beginning, each side might have been more patient and much wiser. Life and history, and right and wrong and the minds of men look out of more windows than we used to think! Did you never hear of the shield that had two sides and both were precious metal?" There was, of course, no lack of honor on either side in the fateful surrender at Appomattox. And Johnston captured an honest soldiers' sentiment that had reverberated

"There was a right side and a wrong side in the late war that no sentiment ought to cause us to forget."

Frederick Douglass, former slave and abolitionist/orator, May 30, 1878

through veterans' memories for decades by 1912. But outside of this pathos and this social need to believe that no one was wrong and everyone was right by their acts of devotion, another process was at work—the denigration of African American dignity and humanity in the Jim Crow system designed to maintain racial segregation and white supremacy, and the attempted erasure of emancipation from the national memory of what the war had been about.

America's Civil War battlefields are sacred ground; they are places that can teach us that bravery came in many forms in the Civil War era. It was the massive sacrifice of life at those sites that gave Frederick Douglass cause, in 1864, to declare "national regeneration" as the "sacred significance" of the war. Douglass imagined a "new order" emerging from the death and destruction, rooted in the brave dream of a society devoted to human equality. If Appomattox is a place where we can reflect on the ending of the Civil War and the tortured story of Reconstruction and national reunion, it can also be a place where we ponder the expansion of freedom for all Americans made possible by the war.

Emancipation and citizenship did not mean freedom and independence for all former slaves. Most lacked money, jobs, or land, and those unable to subsist on their own might find themselves living on their old plantation and working for the same overseer—the only difference being that now they might be paid a meager wage or a share of the crop. All in all, their lives would be little different than the lives of those seen here in this 1860 photograph of slaves on a South Carolina cotton plantation bringing in the day's pickings.

Part 4

Guide to the Park

From Battlefield to Park

Appomattox Court House was originally known as Clover Hill, a small settlement of just a few houses around the tavern, which was a stopping-off point on the main Richmond-Lynchburg Stage Road. When Appomattox County was formed in 1845, Clover Hill was chosen as the county seat and the town was renamed. After the county courthouse was built in 1846 the settlement grew into a village of homes, stores, and lawyers' offices. Appomattox Court House National Historical Park represents the appearance of the village on April 9, 1865, when Robert E. Lee surrendered to Ulysses S. Grant.

When the opposing armies left Appomattox Court House, the village settled back into obscurity, apparently forgotten in the rush to mark battlefields, large and small of the late war. In 1889 a group of Union veterans, organized as the Appomattox Land Company, planned to develop the area, but these plans were soon shattered. The McLean House was bought with the intention of moving it, and in 1892 the courthouse burned to the ground. The village's future had gone up in smoke.

In the next 40 years only a Congressional resolution in 1895 and the dedication of the North Carolina monument in 1905 disturbed the stillness. On June 18, 1930, Congress passed a bill providing for the building of a monument on the old courthouse grounds to memorialize the surrender. In July 1933 this responsibility was transferred to the National Park Service, which took the opportunity to suggest restoring the whole village. The idea was enthusiastically received locally and soon won national support. The program was carried to Congress and in 1935 President Franklin D. Roosevelt signed a bill creating Appomattox Court House National Monument. (The designation was changed to national historical park in 1954.) The Resettlement Administration began purchasing land, and in 1940, the park was proclaimed established. Work on the buildings started, but it was interrupted by World War II.

After the war, the work of restoration and reconstruction was revived and slowly the buildings were opened. Today little work remains to be done, and, with the exception of those buildings that have not been reconstructed, the village looks very much as it did the day Grant and Lee took the first steps in reuniting the United States.

Visiting the Village Today

Here on April 9, 1865, in the house at the extreme right in the photograph on these pages, Robert E. Lee surrendered his Army of Northern Virginia to Ulysses S. Grant, general in chief of all United States forces, marking for all intents and purposes the end of the Southern states' attempt to create a separate nation. No photograph shows the village in 1865. The inset below was taken in 1889 from approximately the same direction as the larger photograph, but farther back and to the right. This is also the view Grant would have had as he approached the McLean house on April 9, 1865.

The National Park Service invites you to walk through the village along the old country lanes and imagine the activity of those April days when Lee's veterans laid down their flags, stacked their weapons, and began the journey back to their homes. Some structures that were standing in 1865 are now gone, victims of time and neglect, but all buildings that figured prominently in the events of the surrender have either been restored or reconstructed. Their locations are noted on the map on pages 110-111.

Outside the village are several other sites you may wish to see while you are at the park. To the northeast, off Va. 24, is the site of Lee's headquarters, where, on the evening of April 8, he pondered his decision to meet with Grant. West of the village, also off Va. 24, is the site of Grant's headquarters for the night of April 9, 1865. Check at the park visitor center for information about how to reach these sites.

Appomattox Court House National Historical Park is located in south central Virginia between Richmond and Lynchburg on Va. 24 northeast of the town of Appomattox. Access is by private car or bus. The nearest major airport is in Richmond. Lynchburg and Richmond are the nearest rail passenger stops. There are motels in Appomattox and a campground at Holliday Lake State Park to the northeast off Va. 24.

For More Information
Appomattox Court House National Historical Park
P.O. Box 218
Appomattox, VA 24522
434-352-8797
www.nps.gov/apco

To learn more about other parks in the National Park System, visit www.nps.gov on the Internet.

Appomattox Court House National Historical Park

The following pages contain a guide to the restored and reconstructed buildings of the village that are shown on the map below. All are within easy walking distance and there is no established order to follow. Information about walking trails to points of interest outside the village is available at the visitor cen-

ter, where knowledgeable National Park Service staff will be glad to answer your questions about the village and its people and the events that took place here. Enjoy yourself, at any season, as you discover this quiet, peaceful, and special place, where the nation began the process of becoming one again.

Note: The roads shown on this map, with the exception of the parking lot, are for pedestrian use only. The faded and numbered buildings represent structures that stood in the village at the time of the surrender but which no longer exist. They are identified at right.

24

Peers House

Richmond - Lynchburg Stage Road

23
22
21
20
19
25

15
16
14
17
18

Clover Hill Tavern

Slave Quarters (restrooms)

Tavern Kitchen (bookstore)

13
12
11

Appomattox County Jail

Visitor Center
Appomattox County Courthouse

Woodson Law Office

Tavern Guesthouse
10 9 8

6

Meeks Stable

Storehouse

Plunkett-Meeks Store

7

3

McLean House

Kitchen

1

2

4

Slave Quarters

5

1 Union Academy Dwelling House
2 Woodson Law Office (1865)
3 Raine Tavern (empty ca. 1865)
4 McLean Smokehouse
5 McLean Stable
6 Pryor Wright House
7 Meeks Storehouse (1865)
8 Office
9 Office
10 Office
11 Tavern Smokehouse
12 Tavern Dining Room
13 Tavern Bar
14 Carriage House
15 Mule Stable
16 Clover Hill Tavern Stable
17 Robertson-Glover Store
18 Original Jail
19 W. Rosser Tenant House
20 W. Rosser Wheelwright Shop
21 W. Rosser Blacksmith Shop
22 W. Rosser Corn Crib
23 W. Rosser Barn
24 Peers Stable
25 Bocock-Isbell Law Office
26 Inge House
27 Peers Cabin/Slave Quarters
28 Moffitt-Layne House
29 Union Academy Hall
30 J. Rosser Blacksmith Shop
31 Wright Stable

Jones Law Office

Prince Edward Court House Road

Bocock-Isbell House

Stable

Kitchen

Bocock Lane

Smokehouse

Back Lane

Mariah Wright House

27

28

26

30

29

31

The furnishings in the house are typical of the McLean's own possessions; some items did in fact belong to the fami-ly, such as the horsehair and mahogany Victorian sofa (above), on which Capt. Rob-ert Lincoln, the President's son and a member of Grant's staff, is reported to have sat, and one of two English poly-chrome vases (opposite). Most of the items in the parlor (above), *which has been re-stored to look as it did when Lee and Grant met there, and the dining room (above left) are copies of the originals.*

The McLean House is the park's main attraction. It is a three-story structure with a parlor and a master bedroom on the first floor, two children's bedrooms on the second, and a warming kitchen and dining room on the ground floor. The original house was built in 1848 and purchased by Wilmer McLean in late 1862. After the Lee-Grant meeting, the house was used on April 10 for the Surrender Commissioners' meeting and, over the next few days, as headquarters for Union Maj. Gen. John Gibbon.

The McLeans sold the house in 1867 and moved to Alexandria. Eventually it was sold to M. E. Dunlap of Niagara Falls, New York, who planned to move it to Chicago for the World's Columbian Exposition. This idea never materialized, and Dunlap decided to move the house to Washington, D.C., where it would be on permanent display. In preparation for this move, he had the house dismantled in 1893. This venture also failed and the bricks and wood were never moved. By the time Appomattox Court House was established as a national historical monument in 1940, time and weather had left only a pile of rotten wood and crumbly bricks. The house was reconstructed based on extensive research and was dedicated in 1950.

Behind the main house are two other structures that are also reconstructions. One is the quarters for the house servants, family slaves. A downstairs room served as the bedroom *(right)*. The other building is the log kit-chen where meals were prepared. The well, inside the gazebo in front of the house, originally was 40 feet deep and, according to old-timers, good even in the dry season. It, too, is a reconstruction.

This one-room, frame building may have been here as early as 1851. John W. Woodson, who was one of several lawyers working in Appomattox Court House, purchased it in 1856 and practiced law here until his death on July 1, 1864, of typhoid. The office is plainly furnished and is typical of country lawyers' offices to be found in Virginia's county seats of that period.

Left: The original Appomattox County courthouse was built in 1846, a year after the county was established. In 1892 fire destroyed the building, and the citizens of the county voted to move the county seat to Appomattox Station, now Appomattox, a five-minute drive southwest. The original courthouse played no role in the surrender. This reconstruction was completed in 1964 and is now used as the park's visitor center.

Above: The Plunkett-Meeks Store was built in 1852 by John Plunkett and was bought in the early 1860s by Francis Meeks, local postmaster and druggist. Meeks's son, who served with the Confederate Army, died of typhoid during the war and is buried near the Meeks Stable *(left)*. The store was one of the social centers of village life. Here neighbors met and argued politics, discussed the latest war news, and exchanged bits of gossip.

Appomattox Court House, Va.,
April 10th, 1865.

THE BEARER, _____ a Paroled Prisoner of the Army of Northern Virginia, has per-
_____ and there remain undisturbed.

Paroles like the one above were printed for issue to Confederate soldiers on a printing press like the one shown at left. In all, 28,231 paroles were printed.

The Clover Hill Tavern dates from 1819 when it was built by Alexander Patteson to serve travelers and stage lines on the Richmond-Lynchburg Stage Road. It came to be the focus of a small collection of homes, stores, and shops that in mid-century were transformed from the settlement of Clover Hill to the village of Appomattox Court House.

An old frame barroom was once located at the southeast corner *(right end)* of the building and a dining room stood at the west *(left)* end. Both are now gone, but are visible in a photograph *(inset above)* taken a few months after Lee's surrender. The paroles for the surrendered Confederates were printed downstairs. The west room has been restored as it appeared in 1865.

Directly behind the tavern are the servants' quarters, where the slaves owned by the tavern keeper lived. Their jobs included cooking and cleaning and perhaps tending a vegetable garden. The building is a reconstruction.

This building, which replaced an earlier one that stood directly across the road, was under construction when the Civil War began and took 10 years to complete. From 1870 until the county seat was moved in 1892 it served as the county jail. The sheriff's office and quarters were on the first floor, and the cells were on the top two. From 1892 until 1940 the building served as the polling station for the Clover Hill magisterial district.

The Clover Hill Tavern guesthouse *(above)* was completed about 1820 and was used to house travelers when the tavern was full. The first floor was often used for storage purposes, and the outside stairs allowed guests access to the other rooms. The tavern kitchen and laundry *(left)* were also completed about 1820 and were convenient to the dining room that stood ahead of it at the west end of the main building. Its upstairs rooms accommodated travelers when there was no room in the tavern or guesthouse.

The Bocock-Isbell House was built by Thomas Salem Bocock and Henry Flood Bocock in 1849-50. Thomas served as speaker of the Confederate House of Representatives from 1862 to 1865, and Henry was the county clerk from 1845 to 1860. A third brother, Willis, was Virginia's attorney general from 1852 to 1857. During the war, the house was occupied by Lewis D. Isbell, who represented the county at the 1861 secession convention and served as the commonwealth's attorney for Appomattox County.

The Jones Law Office was probably built between 1845 and 1860 and was standing at the time of the surrender. This was the office and town home of Crawford Jones, Appomattox County farmer, lawyer, and local secessionist leader. After the war John Robinson, a black shoemaker, and his wife lived here. They are buried in a small graveyard behind the house.

Joel Walker Sweeney

Richard A. Sweeney

Sampson D. Sweeney

Located on the grounds of Appomattox Court House National Historical Park is the home *(below)* of Charles H. Sweeney, cousin of Joel Walker Sweeney, developer and popularizer of the modern five-string banjo. Joel and his brother Richard died before the Civil War began. The youngest brother, Sampson D. Sweeney, along with cousins Charles and Robert Miller Sweeney, joined the Confederate cavalry. Sam and Bob were later detailed to serve on Maj. Gen. J.E.B. Stuart's headquarters staff.

Joel Sweeney, whose banjo is shown on the opposite page, was considered by many to be the dean of minstrel banjoists. He is said to have learned to play banjo from slaves on his father's plantation in Appomattox County, Virginia, and introduced the sound of the instrument to vast numbers of white audiences. In 1831, billed as Sweeney's Minstrels, Sweeney

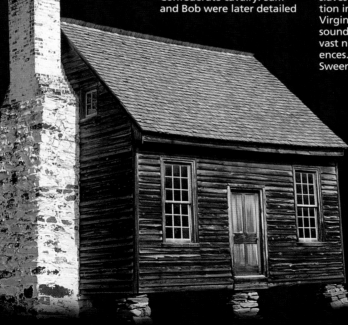

Originally built in the 1830s, the restored Charles Sweeney Cabin is a fine example of a vernacular "hall"-type cabin common in rural Virginia at the time of the Civil War.

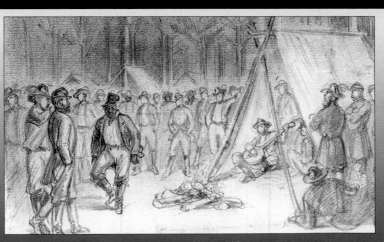

and a group of musicians launched themselves on a series of successful minstrel tours in the United States and abroad that continued until Sweeney's death 29 years later. Joel's younger brothers Richard and Sampson joined the show in the 1850s.

The fame that Sweeney's Minstrels achieved during their years on the stage served Sam Sweeney immeasurably following Joel's death in 1860 and well into the Civil War. As an orderly on Stuart's staff, Sam became perhaps the most famous of Civil War banjoists. It was said that, until Sam's death in January 1864, he could be seen seated near the general's tent on almost any given evening, plunking away on his banjo, and singing the old tunes amongst some of the Confederacy's best and brightest military leaders. One of those evening entertainments was sketched (above) by Frank Vizetelly for the *Illustrated London News* in 1862.

Charles Sweeney served with both the 2nd Virginia Cavalry and the Stuart Horse Artillery during the war. In the final days of the Appomattox Campaign his cabin was used for headquarters by Maj. Gen. William Henry Fitzhugh "Rooney" Lee.

Joel Sweeney's five-string banjo dates from the early 1830s. His initials "J.S." are still faintly visible in the wood. The banjo is now in the Natural History Museum of Los Angeles County, California.

Peers House, Mariah Wright House, and Connor-Sweeney Cabin

At the time of the surrender, this frame residence was the home of the county clerk, George T. Peers, and his family. The house was built sometime before 1855, when Samuel McDearmon sold it to William Abbitt. The last discharges of Confederate artillery on the morning of April 9, 1865, were fired from the Peers' front yard against the Federal Fifth Corps.

This frame house was most likely built in the early to mid-1820s and at the time of the surrender belonged to a widow named Mariah Wright. On the morning of April 9, 1865, Gen. Joshua L. Chamberlain's brigade of Federal Fifth Corps infantry was advancing on the Confederates and his right flank had reached the Wright House when a flag of truce came out from their lines. The house's interior is unfinished.

The Connor-Sweeney Cabin was home to Jennings W. Connor and his bride Missouri Sweeney, who were married in 1865. The house was built sometime between 1860 and 1865. Connor enlisted as a private in the 46th Virginia Infantry on June 18, 1861. He was captured during the Appomattox Campaign at Sailor's Creek on April 6 and was not paroled until July 1, 1865. The building was also used as a hospital after the fighting at Appomattox Court House.

Confederate Cemetery and North Carolina Monument

A single Federal grave is located in the Confederate Cemetery alongside those of one-time foes. This unidentified Union soldier was found in a wooded lot after the other Federal dead had been removed in 1866 and 1867, mostly to Poplar Grove National Cemetery near Petersburg.

Of the 18 Southern soldiers buried in the Confederate Cemetery just west of the village of Appomattox Court House near the old Richmond-Lynchburg Stage Road, only eight are identified. The cemetery was established in 1866 by the Ladies Memorial Association of Appomattox.

This North Carolina Monument was erected in 1905 by veterans from that state on the site where the last volley fired by the Army of Northern Virginia took place. The monument not only recognizes the role of North Carolina troops at Appomattox, it eulogizes their contributions throughout the war, proclaiming them "First at Bethel, farthest to the front at Gettysburg and Chickamauga, and last at Appomattox."

2nd United States Artillery Site and Sweeney Prizery

This artillery piece represents one of the two guns served by Battery A of the 2nd United States Artillery that occupied this position on the morning of April 9, 1865. The guns were supported for a time by a portion of the 1st Maine Cavalry, but were overrun and captured by North Carolina cavalry early in the battle.

The Sweeney Prizery is believed to be one of the oldest structures in the Appomattox area. It was built between 1790 and 1799. It has been covered with tin to protect the original wooden walls. The process of packing tobacco leaf into hogsheads was called prizing and barns where the hogsheads were stored were called prizeries. Gen. Fitzhugh Lee spent part of the night of April 8-9, 1865, in this building.

The Road to Disunion and War

Boritt, Gabor. *Why the Civil War Came.* New York: Oxford University Press, 1996.

Klein, Maury. *Days of Defiance: Sumter, Secession, and the Coming of the Civil War.* New York: Alfred A. Knopf, 1997.

Levine, Bruce. *Half Slave and Half Free: The Roots of the Civil War.* New York: Hill and Wang, 1992.

McPherson, James M. *Battle Cry of Freedom: The Civil War Era.* New York: Ballantine Books, 1988.

Potter, David M. *The Impending Crisis, 1848-1861.* New York: Harper & Row, 1976.

Stampp, Kenneth M., ed. *The Causes of the Civil War.* New York: Touchstone, 1991.

From Petersburg to Appomattox

Bradley, Mark L. *This Astounding Close: The Road to Bennett Place.* Chapel Hill: University of North Carolina Press, 2000.

Calkins, Chris M. *The Appomattox Campaign, March 29-April 9, 1865.* Conshohocken, Pa.: Combined Books, 1997.

_____. *The Battles of Appomattox Station and Appomattox Court House, April 8-9, 1865.* Lynchburg, Va.: H. E. Howard, Inc., 1987.

_____. *The Final Bivouac: The Surrender Parade at Appomattox and the Disbanding of the Armies.* Lynchburg, Va.: H. E. Howard, Inc., 1988.

Catton, Bruce. *A Stillness at Appomattox.* Garden City, N.Y.: Doubleday & Company, 1953.

Cauble, Frank P. *The Proceedings Connected with the Surrender of the Army of Northern Virginia, April 1865.* Lynchburg, Va.: H. E. Howard, Inc., 1987.

Davis, Burke. *To Appomattox: Nine April Days, 1865.* New York: Holt, Rinehart and Winston, 1959.

Freeman, Douglas Southall. *R. E. Lee, A Biography.* 4 vols. New York: Charles Scribner's Sons, 1934-36. Volume 4.

Gallagher, Gary W., ed. *Fighting for the Confederacy: The Personal Recollections of General Edward Porter Alexander.* Chapel Hill: University of North Carolina Press, 1989.

Grant, Ulysses S. *Personal Memoirs.* 2 vols. New York: Charles L. Webster Company, 1886. Volume 2.

Johnson, Robert Underwood, and Clarence Clough Buel, eds. *Battles and Leaders of the Civil War.* 4 vols. New York: The Century Company, 1888. Volume 4.

Maurice, Sir Frederick, ed. *An Aide-de-Camp of Lee: The Papers of Colonel Charles Marshall.* Boston: Little, Brown & Company, 1927.

Nine, William G., and Ronald Wilson. *The Appomattox Paroles, April 9-15, 1865.* Lynchburg, Va.: H. E. Howard, Inc., 1989.

Trudeau, Noah Andre. *Out of the Storm: The End of the Civil War, April 1865.* Boston: Little, Brown & Co., 1994.

Wheeler, Richard. *Witness to Appomattox.* New York: Harper & Row, 1989.

Appomattox: Legacies and Memory

Blight, David W. *Race and Reunion: The Civil War in American Memory.* Cambridge: Harvard University Press, 2001.

Foner, Eric. *A Short History of Reconstruction, 1863-1877.* New York: Harper & Row, 1990.

Foster, Gaines M. *Ghosts of the Confederacy: Defeat, the Lost Cause, and the Emergence of the New South.* New York: Oxford University Press, 1987.

Litwack, Leon F. *Been in the Storm So Long: The Aftermath of Slavery.* New York: Vantage Books, 1980.

Silber, Nina. *The Romance of Reunion: Northerners and the South, 1865-1900.* Chapel Hill: University of North Carolina Press, 1993.

Warren, Robert Penn. *The Legacy of the Civil War: Meditations on the Centennial.* New York: Random House, 1961.

Index
Numbers in italics refer to photographs, illustrations, or maps

☆GPO:2008–339-969/20017 Printed on recycled paper.

Picture Sources